Contemporary COOKING

Volume 10

Contemporary
COOKING

Volume 10

Contemporary Cooking

Editorial production by James Charlton Associates, Ltd.,
New York. Editor-in-Chief, James Charlton; Executive Edi-
tor, Cara DeSilva; Managing Editors, Barbara Binswanger,
Jennie McGregor; Food Editors, Gilda Abramowitz, Helen
Feingold, Judy Knipe, Inez M. Krech, Betsy Lawrence,
Anne Lanigan, Maria Robbins, Susan Sarao, Joan
Whitman; Wine Consultant, Rory Callahan.

Book production and manufacturing consulting by:
Cobb/Dunlop Publishing Services, Inc., New York
Art Direction and interior design by:
Marsha Cohen/Parallelogram
Layout by: Jeanne Borczuk of SOHO Studio, New York
Composition by: Kachina Typesetting, Tempe, Arizona
Cover design by: Koechel/Peterson Design, Minneapolis

Acknowledgments: Pat Cocklin, Delu PAL International,
Alan Duns, John Elliott, Gus Francisco Photography, Mel-
vin Grey, Gina Harris, Anthony Kay, Paul Kemp, David
Levin, David Meldrum, Roger Phillips, Nick Powell, Iain
Reid, John Turner, Paul Williams, George Wright, Cuisin-
arts, Inc.

Printed and bound in Yugoslavia by CGP Delo.

Library of Congress Cataloging in Publication Data
Main entry under title:

Contemporary Cooking.

  Includes index.
  1. Cookery. I. Minnesota Mining and Manufacturing
Company.
TX715.C7586   1984   641.5   84-2563
0-88159-500-4   —   (set)
ISBN: 0-88159-009-6

CONTENTS

for the Contemporary Cooking Series

VOLUME 10

Part One

CANAPÉS AND OTHER FANCY SANDWICHES

In the course of researching the meaning of a particular culinary term it is possible to come across a treasure trove of amusing if not exactly enlightening information. For example, it seems (according to some sources) that the word "canapé" originally meant a canopy or mosquito netting over a couch or a bed. In time—these sources maintain—the word came to mean the couch or bed itself. Then follows a leap of imagination by which we guess that the bite-size pieces of bread or pastry spread with savory edibles are called canapés because they are most often consumed before dinner, that is, while still seated on the living-room couch. Other sources maintain that the word comes directly from the French for couch and before that the Medieval Latin *canapeum.* Perhaps in a flight of culinary fancy the bread itself seemed to provide the bed or couch on which a tasty morsel rested. One authoritative source states: "It is correct to offer canapés to guests in the living room, just before dinner; or as a first course at luncheon or dinner; or at receptions and teas. When canapés or tidbits are served with relishes, the combination is known as an hors d'oeuvre." (*World Famous Chef's Cook Book,* compiled by Ford Naylor)

According to Richard Mariani, the word "canapé" first appeared in print in English in 1890 in reference to a tidbit served with anchovies. (*The Dictionary of American Food and Drink*) From this it might seem that canapés are more or less the same as hors d'oeuvre, but for a further definitional refinement. *The Morris Dictionary of Word and Phrase Origins* quotes an unidentified leading cookbook as follows: "The phrase hors d'oeuvre is used to describe savory little appetizers or relishes other than *canapés.*" Canapés are defined as "savory appetizers made with a bread, cracker or pastry base, so that they can be picked up with the fingers and eaten in one or two bites." After worrying this linguistic enigma a bit further, *The Morris Dictionary* concludes with a warning on pronounciation, citing as an example the awful gaucherie of the newly rich millionaire who wanted to be served a platter of "horses' doovers."

The venerable *Larousse Gastronomique* entirely ignores this etymological hanky panky and states definitively, if somewhat dryly: "The primary meaning of this word [canapé] is a slice of crustless bread, cut in rectangular shapes, the size and thickness of which varies depending on the nature of ingredients to be put on them." If only they had stopped there! But no! Canapés, it seems, are also called *croutons,* and as such they are toasted or fried before they are spread with whatever mixture is put on them. And in this guise they are said to be a classical accompaniment to winged game, spread with the intestines of the birds. Canapés, served as hors d'oeuvre, appear in a secondary position in this hierarchy of culinary definitions. As such they may include not only the abovementioned crustless bread, but also brioche and various pastry cases to serve as the foundation for the savory tidbit they convey from hand to mouth.

All this only seems complicated on the page. Any small child can tell you how to turn some ordinary bread and spread into a fancy tasty tidbit. The rules are few and very simple. The first and most important is that whatever bread you use must have not a trace of crust. Cut all the crust away mercilessly and feed it to the birds. Then the bread must be sliced thin—not so thin that it will fall apart and yet thin enough so that it will not in the least presume to satisfy hunger on its own. The bread must be cut into small pleasing shapes and forms, preferably with a cookie cutter. Whatever is placed or spread on these must be flavorful and attractive. Above all, canapés must look pretty.

This is where all your hours of practice at making radish roses and scallion brushes will finally prove worthwhile.

A close relative of the canapé is the Danish smørrebrød, the lovely open-face sandwiches of which there are hundreds of examples. Actually, in Denmark, smørrebrød are often served as a complete meal in themselves, but there are *snitter,* miniature versions of the same grown-up smørrebrød, and these are served before the meal with drinks.

The English, too, took up the canapé/hors d'oeuvre idea but gave it an eccentric twist. The earnest Mrs. Beeton perhaps misunderstood what French chefs meant when they used the word "hors d'oeuvre," which means, quite literally, "outside the main design of the meal," and so she placed these "savouries" last on the English menus, coming after the sweet and the coffee. This must have been a startling jolt to all the French gourmets and certainly helped reinforce the Gallic notion of England as a nation gastronomically retarded. Today most English savories are served before the meal, but one does still hear of the amazement of a foreign diner faced with a pungent triangle of anchovy toast right after he has done full justice to a luscious raspberry fool.

In America we serve canapés and fancy sandwiches on any number of occasions. It is useful to keep your freezer, refrigerator and pantry stocked with the makings of an assortment of these dainty tidbits. Whether you serve them with cocktails or tea, for brunch or as a midnight snack, a platter of quickly assembled canapés allows you to make any occasion a special occasion.

CANAPÉS AND OTHER FANCY SAND- WICHES

Party sandwiches, canapés, profiteroles and bouchées are all small savory snacks suitable for serving at cocktail parties. Profiteroles and bouchées also make good appetizers. Sandwiches and canapés are made with a bread base—canapés can also be made with crackers—and an infinite variety of fillings and toppings. Profiteroles (cream puffs) are small balls of baked *pâte à choux* (see Volume 4 Index) that are split and stuffed with a creamy filling. Bouchées, the most elegant of this group, are puff-pastry cases usually filled with creamed food and served hot or cold.

Party Sandwiches

Ingredients. A party sandwich may be as simple as a miniature version of a regular sandwich or as elaborate as a frosted layer cake. But whatever its form, a sandwich will be only as good as its ingredients, and perhaps the most important ingredient is the bread. An unsliced home-style sandwich loaf of white or whole-wheat bread, homemade or from a good bakery, will give the best results. Buying the bread unsliced allows you to control the thickness of the sandwich instead of having it predetermined for you, and for some sandwiches unsliced bread is a requirement because the loaf must be cut into lengthwise slices. For sandwiches in which the bread is stacked in layers, a day-old loaf is best because it has had time to firm up and will not absorb the filling as quickly as freshly baked bread. However, for sandwiches in which the slices are rolled or other-

wise manipulated, the bread must be fresh and supple enough not to tear or crumble as it is being shaped. If you have any doubt about which kind of bread to buy, discuss your requirements with your baker.

Some of our sandwich recipes include both a spread and a filling. The spread, which may be softened butter or cream cheese or thick, preferably homemade, mayonnaise (see Volume 3 Index), acts both as a flavoring and as a barrier between the bread and any moisture in the filling, and, when chilled, as the medium that holds the sandwich together. The spread should always be creamy enough to be

smeared easily so the bread does not tear. Sandwich fillings can range from your favorite tuna fish or egg salad to chopped watercress and mayonnaise to caviar and whipped cream cheese to puréed smoked salmon or mushrooms. In this section, there are several recipes for sandwich fillings alone, and many of the other recipes, including those for profiteroles, contain fillings that can be used for most sandwiches.

Fancy Sandwiches, neatly cut into pretty shapes and spread with well-seasoned fillings, are basically small versions of the traditional sandwich. Use close-grained, day-old white or whole-wheat bread, preferably un-

Rolled Sandwiches

1 Remove all the crusts from the loaf except at one end. Cut the loaf lengthwise into ¼-inch-thick slices. Cover each slice with the spread of your choice.

2 Cut each slice into 3 equal rectangular pieces, keeping the end with the crust still on it facing away from you.

3 Place the filling on the end of the slice nearest you. Roll away from you toward crust end.

4 Pack the rolls open side up in a dish. Cover and chill for 30 minutes in refrigerator before serving.

sliced. Remove the crusts and, if you are using unsliced bread, cut the bread into ¼-inch slices. Cover each slice generously with softened butter or another spread, then sandwich the slices together with the filling.

Using small, fancy pastry cutters that are deep enough not to mash the sandwich, cut through it, making your cuts close together so that you can get as many fancy shapes as possible from one sandwich. If you prefer, use a sharp knife to make squares, diamonds or fingers (long, thin rectangles).

Ribbon Sandwiches are made with alternating slices of white and whole-wheat bread. They tend to be

fragile when they are cut into fingers, so it is essential to use a filling that will firm up when chilled and hold the layers together. (Ribbon sandwiches are always chilled before serving.)

To make ribbon sandwiches, first prepare the filling. For a 3-layer sandwich you may use the same filling throughout or 2 complementary ones. As many as 4 fillings may be used for a 5-layer sandwich. Using day-old bread, cut the crusts from 1 small white loaf and 1 small whole-wheat loaf. Cover the slices with softened butter and then with filling, making sure that the center slices are spread on both sides. Using alternating slices of white and whole-

wheat bread, make a sandwich that is 3 to 5 layers high. Wrap the sandwich tightly in foil and chill for at least 2 hours. Unwrap and, using a long-bladed knife that has been warmed in hot water and wiped dry, cut the sandwich lengthwise into slices 1 inch wide. Cut each slice crosswise into 3 ribbons. Arrange the ribbons carefully on a serving dish. Cover with plastic wrap and refrigerate if you are not serving immediately.

Rolled Sandwiches are very attractive for parties, especially when they are tastefully arranged and garnished. The most celebrated of these is a slice of bread spread with mayonnaise and then rolled around an asparagus tip whose end peeps out of the sandwich.

Rolled sandwiches must be made from a very fresh unsliced loaf. To cut the bread without tearing it, chill the loaf and use a warmed knife. Trim all the crusts from the loaf, except from one short end. Cut the bread lengthwise into ¼-inch-thick slices. Cover with softened butter or cream cheese or thick mayonnaise, making sure that the spread is taken right to the edges of the bread. Then cut each slice lengthwise into 3 equal rectangles. Arrange the rectangles so that the crust end faces away from you and place the filling on the end nearest you. Roll up the sandwich toward the crust end. Place the rolls in a dish, cut side up. Pack them in so that they do not unroll, but not so tightly that they will lose their shape. Cover the dish with aluminum foil or plastic wrap and chill for at least 30 minutes before serving.

Pinwheels are a variation of rolled sandwiches. You will need a fresh, unsliced sandwich loaf and a filling that is soft and easy to spread. Start by removing all the crusts, cutting off the bottom crust last. Square up the loaf as you cut so that the top is the same size as the base. Carefully cut the loaf along its length into slices ¼ inch thick. Spread each slice with softened butter or cream cheese or thick mayonnaise, then spread with the filling you've chosen, making sure both the spread and filling reach right to the

Pinwheel Sandwiches

1 Trim away crusts from bread, cutting loaf into a neat rectangle. Cut loaf lengthwise into ¼-inch-thick slices. Cover each slice evenly with spread.

2 Cover each slice with the filling of your choice and place slice on a clean kitchen towel.

3 Using the towel as an aid, carefully roll the slice tightly from one short end to the other to make a roll.

4 Wrap the roll securely in foil and chill in the refrigerator for 30 minutes. Remove foil and cut roll into slices.

Horns

1 Remove crusts and cut bread into thin slices. Cover slices with a thin layer of butter or another spread.

2 Round one corner of each slice.

3 Spread each slice with a thin layer of filling. Bring up the corners at the sides of the base so they overlap.

4 Press edges together to seal; then secure with a toothpick and chill. When ready to serve, remove toothpicks and fill horns with remaining filling.

edges of the bread. Place one of the slices of bread, filling side up, on a clean kitchen towel, and, using the towel as an aid, carefully roll the slice from one short end to the other to make a plump tight roll. Wrap the roll securely in foil or plastic wrap and refrigerate for at least 30 minutes before serving. Chilling will firm up the ingredients, preventing the slices from unwinding after the pinwheels are cut. Proceed with the remaining slices in the same way. When ready to serve, remove the foil and place the roll, seam side down, on a board. Using a sharp knife, cut the roll into slices ¾ inch thick. Arrange the pinwheels in an overlapping pattern on a serving plate.

Horns are cone-shaped sandwiches filled with a soft, creamy spread, such as a pâté or a cream cheese mixture. Use a fresh, unsliced sandwich loaf. Remove all the crusts and cut crosswise into ¼-inch-thick slices (the thinner the slices the easier to shape). Using a plain round pastry cutter or a sharp knife, round off one corner of each slice. Spread the slices with butter and then, reserving about one third of the filling for later use, top the slices with a thin layer of the filling. Now shape the horns. The rounded corner will be the base of the horn. Bring up the sharp corners at either side of the base and overlap them in the center to

Making a Fried Canapé Base

1 For each canapé, take a slice of firm, fresh bread about ⅓ inch thick.

2 Remove crusts from sliced bread and cut into desired shapes.

3 Heat required amount of oil and butter in a skillet over medium heat.

Sandwich Cake

1 Remove crusts from a day-old loaf, level top and cut the loaf into 3 or 4 horizontal layers.

2 Butter the layers, spreading all but the outside layers on both sides. Divide filling, then spread over bread, beginning with bottom slice. Top with next slice.

3 Continue to spread and sandwich layers until all the slices are in place. Press gently to secure. Chill 2 hours or until set.

4 Cover cake completely with a savory, creamy spread and garnish to complement filling.

4 When butter has melted, fry bread slices for about 3 minutes on each side, or until crisp. Watch to see that they do not burn.

5 Drain the bread slices on paper towels and keep them hot until needed.

make a cone shape. Gently press the bread together where it overlaps, then fasten the overlap with a toothpick. Transfer the horns to a plate, setting them close together. Cover and place in the refrigerator for at least 30 minutes, or until the spread and filling are firm. When ready to serve, carefully remove the toothpicks and, holding each cone upright, fill the horns with the remaining filling.

Sandwich Loaves, or Cakes resemble sweet cakes, but the layers are make of bread and savory ingredients that are used for the filling and decoration. The loaves are beautiful to look at and make a charming centerpiece for a buffet table or a cocktail party.

To make a sandwich cake, use a soft round loaf or a rectangular sandwich loaf of day-old bread. Remove the crusts and cut the loaf horizontally into 3 or 4 layers. Spread each layer with butter, buttering all but the outside layers on both sides. Spread the layers with the fillings and sandwich them together. Press the loaf down gently to secure. Round sandwich loaves may be decorated immediately, but because rectangular loaves tend to be more fragile, they should be tightly wrapped and chilled for at least 2 hours before they are decorated and sliced. "Frost" with a creamy mixture that is easy to spread—cream cheese, thick mayonnaise, and puréed cottage cheese are all suitable coatings. Spread the coating all over the top and sides of the loaf until the bread is completely hidden. Garnish the top and sides to complement the filling. Tomato wedges, gherkin fans, slices of olive or hard-cooked eggs all look attractive. To serve, cut a round loaf into wedges and a rectangular one into thin slices.

Storing Party Sandwiches Overnight. If securely wrapped in aluminum foil or plastic wrap as soon as they are made, most sandwiches may be kept for 24 hours in the refrigerator. This is not true, however, for open sandwiches or cones, which become limp and dry out quickly. Wrap sandwiches of different flavors separately.

8

Ribbon and pinwheel sandwiches are best stored as a block, ready for slicing. Sandwich cakes and loaves should be stored undecorated.

Freezing Party Sandwiches. Well-wrapped in plastic wrap and stored in freezer containers, many sandwiches may be frozen for up to 2 months, provided the fillings are suitable for freezing. Sandwiches that contain hard-cooked eggs, mayonnaise, salad greens, jams, or preserves should not be frozen. Freeze ribbons and pinwheels in unsliced blocks, and stack cut sandwiches tightly. Freeze decorated cakes and loaves unwrapped, then place them in freezer containers for storage. Thaw sandwiches in their wrappings in the refrigerator or at room temperature. For loaves, remove the lids from the containers. Pinwheels and ribbon sandwiches will be easier to slice while they are still partly frozen; cover slices loosely and allow sandwiches to finish thawing.

Canapés

Canapés are small, dainty, open sandwiches that are served hot or cold as cocktail snacks or appetizers. The toppings should be colorful and tasty. They may include cheese, meat, eggs, fish and vegetables, alone or in combination, plus a wide range of seasonings, herbs, and spices. The many possibilities allow you to give full rein to your imagination when composing a tray of canapés for a cocktail party. The canapé base is traditionally bread that is left plain, toasted, or fried, but may also be a cracker. Use sliced bakery white and whole-wheat bread or packaged thinly sliced rye or pumpernickel bread, which are easy to cut into small pieces. If the bread base is not going to be toasted or fried, use day-old bread, which is firmer and will not absorb moisture as quickly as fresh bread. For toasted and fried bases, use fresh bread. All toasting should be done in the broiler.

Advance preparation of canapés varies from recipe to recipe. As a rule, it is best to prepare the topping in ad-

Filled Profiteroles (see Index for recipes)

Cream Cheese and Nut Filling

Chicken and Mushroom Filling

Pâté Filling

Ham and Chutney Filling

Filling Baked Bouchée Cases

1 With the point of a sharp knife, ease away the pastry lid in the center of the case and scrape away any soft, damp pastry inside.

2 Fill the bouchées, using a teaspoon. Heap filling slightly, but do not let it overflow. Top with the pastry lid removed earlier.

Tongue Filling

Waldorf Filling

Smoked Trout Filling

Shrimp Filling

Ham and Asparagus Filling

Smoked Salmon Filling

vance and finish assembling the canapés close to serving time. Canapés that are to be served cold may be made several hours in advance, placed on a dish, carefully covered with foil so as not to disturb the toppings, and left in the refrigerator for several hours. Canapés do not freeze well because they cannot be wrapped tightly enough to protect them without squashing the toppings.

Cocktail Profiteroles (Cream Puffs)

Tiny cream puffs, 1¼ to 1½ inches in diameter, may be filled with well-flavored savory mixtures and served as delicious cocktail party food. To make the puffs, follow the pâte à choux recipe for 24 profiteroles (see Volume 4 Index), omitting the teaspoon of sugar. When the profiteroles have been baked, cooled, and oven-dried as directed, split the puffs and gently scrape out any moist dough with the tip of a spoon, then fill them with as much savory mixture as they will hold. Soft fillings may be put into a pastry bag and piped into the puffs; stiffer mixtures, and those that contain coarsely chopped ingredients, should be spooned in. Savory profiterole fillings are based on highly seasoned cream cheese, mayonnaise, béchamel sauce or whipped or sour cream, and may include puréed fish or very finely chopped meat, cheese or vegetables. It is best to make the filling in advance and fill the puffs close to serving time so that the pastry does not become soggy.

Bouchées

Bouchées are small puff-pastry cases, about 1½ inches in diameter, filled with savory mixtures, and served hot or cold. To make them, follow one of the puff pastry recipes (see Volume 5 Index) and shape and bake the pastry following the bouchée instructions. For cold or room-temperature appetizers, prepare one of the profiterole filling recipes (see Index). For hot fillings, use a finely diced mixture with a sauce, or any of the recipes that follow. To prepare the cases for filling, use the tip of a sharp knife to ease away the small round in the center of the bouchée; reserve the round to use as a lid. If there is any soft damp dough in the case, remove it gently with the knife tip or a teaspoon. Spoon filling into the case; mound the filling, but do not allow it to spill over the sides. Replace the pastry lid and, if required, reheat the bouchées for about 10 minutes in a preheated 425°F oven. Serve filled bouchées as soon as possible because the pastry will lose its crispness.

Mushroom Sandwich Filling

makes about 2 cups

8	ounces cream cheese, at room temperature		2	tablespoons chopped fresh chives
½	teaspoon salt		2	hard-cooked eggs
¼	teaspoon freshly ground black pepper		1	small dill pickle
			2	ounces mushrooms

Combine the cream cheese, salt, pepper and chives in a mixing bowl and mash to blend. Shell the eggs, chop fine, and add to bowl. Mince the pickle and add. Trim the bottoms of the mushroom stems, wipe the mushrooms clean with damp cloth or paper towel, and chop fine. Add to the mixing bowl. Combine ingredients thoroughly. Cover the bowl with aluminum foil and store in the refrigerator for up to 3 days.

Veal and Anchovy Sandwich Filling

makes about 1¼ cups

1	cup boneless cooked veal		1	lemon
2	anchovy fillets		3	to 4 grindings of black pepper
3	tablespoons Mayonnaise (see Volume 3 Index)		2	teaspoons drained chopped capers

Cut the veal into 1-inch pieces and place in a food processor fitted with the steel blade. Drain the anchovy fillets and add them to the veal together with the mayonnaise, 1 teaspoon lemon juice and pepper. Process until the mixture is puréed. Or put the veal through the fine blade of a meat grinder, chop the anchovies very fine, and combine with mayonnaise and pepper. Turn into a small bowl and stir in the capers. Store in a tightly covered small container in the refrigerator for up to 24 hours.

Goat Cheese Sandwich Filling

makes about 1 cup

8	ounces goat cheese, at room temperature		1	tablespoon chopped fresh tarragon, or 1 teaspoon dried tarragon
3	to 4 tablespoons heavy cream		3	to 4 grindings black pepper

In a mixing bowl, cream the goat cheese with a spoon. When the cheese is smooth, stir in enough cream to make a light, spreadable mixture. Add the tarragon and pepper and mix well. Store in a well-covered small container in the refrigerator for up to 3 days. Return to room temperature before using.

Open Sandwich Cakes

16 sandwiches

	Beef filling			Caviar filling
4	ounces chipped beef		1	hard-cooked egg
4	ounces butter, at room temperature		¼	cup Mayonnaise (see Volume 3 Index)
1	tablespoon Dijon-style mustard		2	tablespoons chopped fresh dill (optional)
			4	tablespoons black caviar or lumpfish roe

Cheese filling

4   ounces cream cheese, at
room temperature
1   tablespoon paprika
2   tablespoons dairy sour cream
1   teaspoon brandy
1   tablespoon finely chopped
fresh chives or finely
chopped onion

Bread

1   day-old light rye sandwich
loaf
1   day-old dark rye sandwich
loaf

To prepare the beef filling, finely chop the chipped beef, either by hand or in a food processor fitted with the steel blade. In a small mixing bowl, cream the butter with a wooden spoon. When it is smooth, beat in the mustard and stir in the beef. Set aside.

To make the caviar filling, shell the hard-cooked egg and chop it fine. Place in a fine-mesh sieve and, using the back of a wooden spoon, rub the egg through the sieve into a mixing bowl. Add the mayonnaise and dill, if you are using it, and gently stir in the caviar. Reserve.

To make the cheese filling, place all the ingredients in a mixing bowl and beat with a wooden spoon until light and creamy. Set aside.

Turn the bread sideways and cut 4 thin lengthwise slices from the center of each loaf. Reserve the remaining bread for another use. Trim the crusts from the slices. Place 1 slice of light rye bread on a serving plate and spread the bread evenly with half the beef mixture. Spread half the caviar filling on a slice of dark rye bread and place over the beef. Spread half the cream cheese filling over a slice of light rye, place on top of the caviar mixture, and finish the cake with a slice of dark rye bread. Set aside. Make a second open sandwich cake in the same way, using the remaining ingredients. Wrap the cakes in aluminum foil or plastic wrap and chill for 2 hours in the refrigerator.

When ready to serve, remove from the refrigerator. With a sharp knife, cut the cake crosswise into thin slices and serve at once.

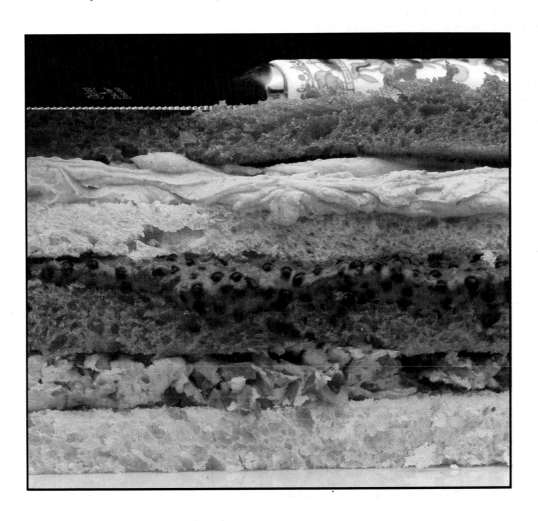

Blue Cheese Pinwheel Sandwiches

20 sandwiches

5 ounces Stilton, Roquefort, or other blue cheese, at room temperature
3 ounces cream cheese, at room temperature
7 tablespoons dairy sour cream
2 tablespoons finely chopped walnuts

pinch of cayenne pepper
1 fresh, unsliced, long whole-wheat sandwich loaf, chilled
4 to 6 ounces unsalted butter, at room temperature

Remove the rind from the blue cheese and crumble it into the bowl of a food processor fitted with the steel blade. Add the cream cheese and sour cream and process until the mixture is a smooth purée. Or blend the cheeses by hand. Turn the mixture into a small bowl and stir in the walnuts and cayenne. Reserve.

With a warmed thin-bladed knife, cut all the crusts from the loaf, removing the bottom crust last, and cutting so that the loaf is uniform in shape. Cut the bread lengthwise into ¼-inch-thick rectangular slices. Spread each slice with but-

ter and then with the blue cheese filling, making sure that the butter and filling extend right to the edges. Place a slice, filling side up, on a clean kitchen towel. Using the towel to help you, roll up the slice starting from the short end nearest you and rolling toward the other. Wrap the roll in aluminum foil or plastic wrap. Roll the remaining slices in the same way. Chill the wrapped rolls in the refrigerator for at least 30 minutes.

To serve, unwrap and place, seam side down, on a wooden board. Cut each roll into 4 thick slices and arrange the slices in an overlapping pattern on a serving plate.

Seafood Sandwich Loaf

12 sandwich Wedges

3½ ounces canned tuna fish
2 tablespoons Tartar sauce or Mayonnaise (see Volume 3 Index)
4 ounces cooked shrimps
2 tablespoons blanched almonds
14 ounces cream cheese, at room temperature
1 lemon
4 ounces skinless, boneless sardines
1 tablespoon tomato paste

2 teaspoons chopped fresh parsley
freshly ground black pepper
salt
1 day-old, unsliced, small white or whole-wheat round loaf
4 tablespoons unsalted butter, at room temperature
4 pitted green olives stuffed with pimento
2 ounces rolled anchovy fillets

Make the fillings. Drain the tuna fish and flake it into a bowl. Add the tartar sauce or mayonnaise and mix until well combined. Set aside. Shell the shrimps, devein them if you wish, and chop into small pieces. Finely chop the almonds. In a small bowl, beat 4 tablespoons (2 ounces) of the cream cheese until smooth. Squeeze the lemon to measure 1 teaspoon. Add the shrimps, almonds, and lemon juice and mix until well combined. Set aside. Drain the sardines, place in a bowl, and mash with a fork. Add the tomato paste, parsley and 2 to 3 grindings of black pepper. Mix well. Taste for seasoning and, if necessary, add salt. Set aside.

Trim the crusts from the bread, leveling top and cutting off the bottom crust last. Cut loaf crosswise into 4 even layers. Spread each layer of bread with the butter, covering both sides of all but the outside pieces. Spread the bottom layer evenly with the sardine filling. Top with the next layer of bread and spread the shrimp mixture over it. Place the third slice of bread over the shrimp and spread with the tuna filling. Cover with the top slice of bread, butter side down. Lightly press the top of the loaf to secure the layers, then wrap the loaf securely in aluminum foil or plastic wrap and refrigerate for 2 hours to allow the fillings to set.

When ready to serve, unwrap the cake and place on a serving dish. To protect the dish during the decorating process, position pieces of wax paper under the cake, along its edges. Beat the remaining cream cheese until smooth and spreadable. Coat the top and sides of the cake with the cheese. Thoroughly drain the olives, slice crosswise, and use center slices to decorate the top of the cake. Thoroughly drain anchovies and use to decorate the base of cake.

Present the cake to your guests, and then, using a sharp, long-bladed knife, cut it into wedges and serve.
Variation: For a more luxurious loaf, use 4 ounces cooked, boneless, fresh salmon in place of the tuna. Instead of the sardine filling, spread 4 ounces of red salmon roe over the bottom layer of bread and sprinkle with lemon juice. Omit the anchovy decoration, and use thin strips of smoked salmon to make a lattice pattern.

Sardine Canapés

16 canapés

4	slices day-old white bread
2	tablespoons unsalted butter, at room temperature
1	lemon
4	ounces skinless, boneless sardines

¼	teaspoon freshly ground black pepper
2	teaspoons minced parsley
3	hard-cooked eggs
16	rolled anchovy fillets

Trim the crusts from the bread, butter the slices, and cut each slice into 4 squares. Squeeze the lemon to measure ½ teaspoon juice.

In a small bowl, mash the sardines, pepper and lemon juice to a paste. Stir in the parsley. Spread the mixture on the squares of bread. Shell the hard-cooked eggs and slice them thin. Place a center slice of egg over each canapé and top with a rolled anchovy fillet. If made in advance, place on a plate, cover with foil, and refrigerate until serving time.

Spicy Horns

16 to 18 horns

12	ounces cottage cheese
1	tablespoon mango chutney
3	to 4 scallions
3	tablespoons Mayonnaise
	(see Volume 3 Index)
1½	teaspoons curry powder

	pinch of cayenne pepper
1	lemon
1	fresh, unsliced, small
	whole-wheat sandwich loaf
4	ounces butter, at room
	temperature

Purée the cottage cheese in a food processor, using the steel blade, then scrape the cheese into a mixing bowl; or use the back of a wooden spoon to press the cheese through a fine sieve into the bowl. Finely chop the fruit in the chutney. Trim the scallions, wash, dry, and chop fine. Add the chutney, scallions, mayonnaise, curry powder, cayenne pepper, and a squeeze of lemon juice to the cheese and stir until well combined. Set aside.

Trim all the crusts from the bread, removing the bottom crust last, and cutting so that the loaf is uniform in shape. Cut loaf crosswise into 16 to 18 ¼-inch-thick slices. Round one corner of each slice, using a curved pastry cutter or a sharp knife. Reserving about one third of the filling, spread each slice with butter and then with 2 teaspoons of the cheese filling. For each horn, bring up the corners at either side of the round end of the slice and overlap the corners in the center to make a cone shape. Press together gently to seal, then secure with a toothpick. Pack the horns tightly into a dish, taking care not to mash them out of shape. Cover the dish with aluminum foil or plastic wrap, and refrigerate for at least 30 minutes.

To serve, remove the cones from the dish and pull out the toothpicks. Hold each horn upright and fill with a portion of the remaining cheese mixture. Arrange on a dish and serve.

Variation: For pâté horns, purée 12 ounces soft liver pâté and ¼ cup heavy cream in a food processor or combine by hand. Stir in 3 to 4 tablespoons finely chopped scallions and 1 or 2 teaspoons of brandy. Fill and shape the horns as instructed.

Hot Spinach and Cheese Canapés

These canapés may be prepared several hours in advance and reheated under the broiler just before serving.

24 canapés

1½   pounds fresh spinach, or
       1½ ten-ounce packages
       frozen chopped spinach
3   ounces Gruyère cheese
4   ounces butter

½   teaspoon freshly ground
      black pepper
    salt
6   slices fresh white bread
2   tablespoons olive oil
⅓   cup fine, dry white bread crumbs

Trim and discard the stems from the fresh spinach and wash the leaves well in several changes of water. Place in a large pan, cover, and steam over medium heat just in the water clinging to the leaves until the spinach wilts completely. Drain the cooked spinach and refresh it under cold running water. Drain it again and squeeze the water from it, a handful at a time. It should be fairly dry. Chop the spinach fine, either by hand or in a food processor fitted with the steel blade. If you are using frozen spinach, cook it according to the package directions. The spinach may be prepared up to a day ahead and kept in a well-covered container in the refrigerator.

Preheat the broiler. Grate the Gruyère cheese—you should have about ¾ cup. Place the spinach in a medium-size saucepan, add 2 tablespoons of the butter and the pepper, and cook over low heat until the spinach is hot,

stirring often. Stir in ½ cup of the cheese, add salt to taste, cover the pan, and set aside in a warm place.

Trim the crusts from the bread and cut each slice diagonally into 4 triangles. Place the olive oil and 4 tablespoons of the butter in a large skillet and set over medium heat. When the butter has melted, add the bread triangles and fry until lightly browned on both sides. Remove the bread from the pan with a slotted spatula and place on paper towels to drain.

Spread 1 tablespoon of the spinach and cheese mixture over each bread triangle. Sprinkle the top of each with the remaining cheese and the bread crumbs. Melt the remaining 2 tablespoons of butter and drizzle it over the tops of the canapés. Arrange them on a baking sheet and place under the broiler for 2 to 3 minutes, or until the canapés are hot and the cheese is lightly browned. Serve at once.

Ham Bouchées

24 bouchées

3   ounces mushrooms
6   ounces boiled ham, in one
      piece
1½   tablespoons unsalted butter
⅞   cup Béchamel Sauce (see
      Volume 3 Index)

¾   teaspoon Dijon-style
      mustard
    pinch of salt
    freshly ground white pepper
24   baked 1½-inch Bouchée
      cases (see Volume 5 Index)

Remove the stems from the mushrooms and wipe the caps with a damp paper towel. Cut the mushrooms into ¼-inch-thick slices. Cut the ham into ¼-inch dice.

In a medium-size saucepan, melt the butter over medium heat. Add the mushrooms and cook for 5 to 6 minutes, or until they have softened slightly, shaking the pan occasionally so the mushrooms do not stick. Stir in the diced ham, béchamel sauce, mustard, salt, and pepper.

Increase the heat to medium and cook the mixture, stirring constantly, for about 5 minutes. The sauce may be prepared in advance to this point. Cover the pan and leave it at room temperature.

Preheat the oven to 425°F. To prepare the bouchée cases for filling, lift out the small dough lids with the point of a sharp knife, and set aside. Scoop out any moist pastry with the knife point or a teaspoon. Place the bouchées on a baking sheet and spoon the ham mixture into them, filling the cases almost to overflowing. (Leftover filling may be used as a topping for baked potatoes, served with hot biscuits, or used as an omelet filling.) Replace the lids on the cases and bake the bouchées for about 10 minutes, or until they are very hot. Serve at once.

Hot Spiced Shrimp Canapés

12 canapés

4	ounces shrimps	1/8	teaspoon cayenne pepper	
4	slices fresh white bread	1/4	teaspoon salt	
1	tablespoon vegetable oil	1	lemon	
4	ounces butter	2	tablespoons chopped parsley	
1/4	teaspoon curry powder			

Shell the shrimps, devein them if you wish, and cut them into 1/2-inch pieces. Set aside.

Trim the crusts from the bread and cut each slice into 3 ovals or 3 fingers. Place the oil and 4 tablespoons of the butter in a large skillet and set over medium heat. When the butter has melted and the mixture is foaming, add the bread and cook until it is crisp and lightly browned on both sides. Watch carefully to be sure that the fingers do not burn.

Remove from the pan with a slotted spatula and drain on several layers of paper towels. Keep warm.

In a small saucepan, melt the remaining 4 tablespoons of butter over medium-low heat. Add the reserved shrimps, curry powder, cayenne pepper, salt and about 1 1/2 teaspoons lemon juice. Simmer gently 2 to 3 minutes until the shrimps are cooked. With a slotted spoon, remove the shrimps from the pan, let them drain slightly, and place them on the bread. Sprinkle each canapé with parsley and serve hot.

Lobster Canapés

18 canapés

1	tablespoon white wine vinegar	1	slice lean bacon	
3	tablespoons olive oil	1	rib celery	
1/4	teaspoon sugar	1	tablespoon chopped parsley	
1/4	teaspoon salt	1	teaspoon finely chopped chives	
1/4	teaspoon freshly ground black pepper	1/8	teaspoon cayenne pepper	
4	ounces cooked lobster	4	to 6 tablespoons Mayonnaise (see Volume 3 Index)	
6	slices fresh white bread			

In a small bowl, mix together the vinegar, oil, sugar, salt and pepper. If using fresh lobster, cut it into small dice. If using canned lobster, drain and shred it. Add the lobster to the vinaigrette, mix well, and marinate for at least 1 hour.

Trim the crusts from the bread, cut each slice into 3 fingers, toast and set aside. Fry the bacon until it is brown and crisp, then drain on paper towels. Crumble the bacon and set aside. String the celery, chop fine, and reserve.

Drain the lobster and discard the marinade. Place the lobster in a small mixing bowl; add the bacon, celery, parsley, chives, cayenne pepper, and enough mayonnaise to bind the mixture. Taste for seasoning and add more salt and pepper, if necessary. Spread the mixture on the toast fingers and serve immediately.

Hot Spiced Cheese Canapés

24 canapés

6	slices fresh white bread	4	ounces cream cheese, at room temperature	
1	shallot	1/2	teaspoon Tabasco®	
1	egg			

Preheat the oven to 375°F. Trim the crusts from the bread, cut each slice into 4 squares, toast, and set aside.

Peel and mince the shallot. Crack the egg into a small mixing bowl and beat. Add the cream cheese and

Tabasco and mix with a wooden spoon until light and creamy. Spread the cheese mixture on the toast squares and place the squares on a baking sheet. Bake for 5 to 10 minutes, or until the tops just begin to brown. Serve at once.

Smoked Salmon and Caviar Canapés

24 canapés

6	large slices day-old whole-wheat bread	4	ounces cream cheese, at room temperature
4	ounces thinly sliced smoked salmon	2	lemons
1	small onion	2	ounces black caviar or lumpfish roe
		6	sprigs of parsley

Using a sharp knife, remove the crusts from the bread and cut each slice into 4 diamond shapes. Cut the smoked salmon into 24 pieces. Peel the onion, slice it into rounds, and break up the slices into rings. Spread each slice of bread with cream cheese and then cover with a piece of smoked salmon. Squeeze 1 lemon to measure about 2 tablespoons.

Sprinkle the juice over the smoked salmon and top with an onion ring. Place a tiny dollop of the caviar in the center of each onion ring. Arrange the canapés on a serving dish. Cut the remaining lemon into wedges and garnish the serving dish with the parsley and lemon. Serve at once, or cover with aluminum foil and keep in the refrigerator until serving time.

Devils on Horseback

12 canapés

½	cup dry red wine		6	slices bacon
12	large prunes		3	slices fresh white bread
12	anchovy fillets		1	bunch watercress
12	blanched almonds			

Pour the wine into a small saucepan and bring it to a boil over high heat. Add the prunes to the boiling wine, remove from the heat, and allow to steep for 40 minutes. Return the pan to medium heat and simmer the prunes until almost all the wine has been absorbed. Set the prunes aside, let them cool, and pit them by making a small slit in each prune.

Preheat the oven to 425°F. Drain the anchovy fillets and wrap one around each almond. Stuff the prunes with the wrapped almonds. Cut the bacon slices in half crosswise, wrap a piece around each prune, and secure it with a toothpick. Place the prunes on a baking sheet and bake for 10 minutes.

While the prunes are in the oven, trim the crusts from the bread, cut each slice diagonally into 4 triangles, and toast them. Wash the watercress and dry. Remove the prunes from the oven and place each one on a toast triangle. Arrange the canapés on a warm plate and garnish with the watercress.

Anchovy and Tomato Canapés

12 canapés

1½	ounces canned anchovy fillets		3	plum tomatoes
2	tablespoons olive oil		6	slices fresh white bread
½	lemon		3	ounces cream cheese, at room temperature (optional)
	freshly ground black pepper		2	tablespoons chopped parsley
2	garlic cloves			

Preheat the broiler. Drain the anchovies and place them in a food processor fitted with the steel blade. Add 1 tablespoon of the olive oil, the juice of the lemon, and a few grindings of pepper. Peel the garlic. Begin processing the anchovies. With the motor running, drop the garlic down the feed tube. Continue to process until the mixture is a smooth paste. Or mince the anchovies and garlic to a fine paste, and then beat in the tablespoon olive oil, lemon juice, and pepper. Set aside. Cut twelve ¼-inch slices from the centers of the plum tomatoes and set aside. (Reserve the remaining pieces of tomato for another purpose.)

With a 2-inch cookie or biscuit cutter cut 2 rounds from each slice of bread. Toast the bread lightly in the broiler. Spread the toast rounds with the anchovy paste and top each with a tomato slice. Brush the tomatoes with the remaining tablespoon of oil. Place the canapés on a baking sheet and set under the broiler for about 5 minutes, or until the tomatoes are just cooked and beginning to brown.

If you are using the cream cheese, beat to soften it while the canapés are broiling. Remove the canapés from the oven, top with a rounded teaspoon of the cheese, sprinkle with parsley, and serve at once.

Profiteroles with Cream Cheese and Walnut Filling

24 profiteroles

6	ounces cream cheese, at room temperature		3	tablespoons finely chopped walnuts
3	tablespoons heavy cream		24	baked Profiteroles (see Volume 4 Index)
1	large garlic clove			
1	teaspoon horseradish			

In a mixing bowl, beat the cream cheese until it is light and fluffy. Beat in the heavy cream until the mixture is smooth. Peel the garlic and put it through a garlic press into the cream cheese mixture. Add the horseradish and walnuts and mix well until blended.

Split the profiteroles, carefully scrape out any moist dough with the tip of a spoon, and spoon the filling into the bottom of each one, heaping it slightly. (Leftover filling may be used as a canapé or sandwich spread.) Replace the tops, arrange profiteroles on a plate, and serve.

Profiteroles with Chicken and Mushroom Filling

24 profiteroles

3	medium-size mushrooms			dash of Tabasco
5½	tablespoons butter, at room temperature		1	tablespoon chopped fresh tarragon, or 1 teaspoon dried tarragon
3	ounces cooked, boneless chicken, chilled		24	baked Profiteroles (see Volume 4 Index)
1	lemon			

Trim the bottoms of the mushroom stems. Wipe the caps clean with a damp cloth or paper towels. Chop the mushrooms fine. In a small skillet, melt 1½ tablespoons of the butter over medium heat. Add the mushrooms and sauté, stirring often, until the liquid rendered by the mushrooms has evaporated. Remove from the heat and allow the mushrooms to cool.

Cut the chicken into 1-inch pieces and place in a food processor fitted with the steel blade. Add the cooled mushrooms, the remaining 4 tablespoons butter, a squeeze of lemon juice and the Tabasco. Process until the chicken

and mushrooms are puréed, or chop the chicken and mushrooms almost to a paste and add the butter, lemon juice, and Tabasco. Turn into a bowl and stir in the tarragon. Split the profiteroles and carefully scrape out any moist dough with the tip of a spoon. Spoon the filling into a pastry bag fitted with a small plain nozzle and pipe into the profiteroles. Or spoon the filling into the bottoms, heaping it slightly. (Leftover filling may be used as a sandwich or canapé spread.) Replace the tops, arrange the profiteroles on a dish, and serve.

Profiteroles with Tongue Filling

24 profiteroles

5	ounces cooked tongue	1½	teaspoons Dijon-style mustard
6	tablespoons unsalted butter, at room temperature	1	orange
		24	baked Profiteroles (see Volume 4 Index)

Cut the tongue into 1-inch pieces and place them in a food processor fitted with the steel blade. Add the butter and mustard and process until the tongue is puréed. Or chop the tongue to a paste and add the butter and mustard. Turn the mixture into a bowl. Remove the orange rind in strips and chop fine to measure 1½ tablespoons. Stir into the tongue mixture. Split the profiteroles, carefully scrape out any moist dough with the tip of a spoon, spoon the filling into the bottoms, heaping it slightly, and replace the tops. (Leftover filling may be used as a sandwich or canapé spread.) Place the profiteroles on a dish and serve.

Profiteroles with Waldorf Filling

24 profiteroles

6	ounces cream cheese, at room temperature	1½	tablespoons finely chopped pecans or salted peanuts
1	small rib celery	24	baked Profiteroles (see Volume 4 Index)
¼	small apple		

In a mixing bowl, beat the cream cheese until it is light and fluffy. Cut off and discard the leaves from the celery, string it and chop the rib fine. Peel, core, and finely chop the apple. Add the celery, apple and chopped nuts to the cream cheese and mix well. Split the profiteroles, carefully remove any moist dough with the tip of a spoon, and fill the bottom of each profiterole with the cream cheese mixture, heaping it slightly, then replace the tops. (Leftover filling may be used as a sandwich or canapé spread.) Place the profiteroles on a dish and serve.

Profiteroles with Smoked Trout Filling

24 profiteroles

1	lemon	1½	tablespoons horseradish
6	ounces smoked trout fillets	24	baked Profiteroles (see Volume 4 Index)
2½	tablespoons heavy cream		

Squeeze the lemon to measure 1½ tablespoons juice. Remove the skin from the smoked trout. Place the trout, cream, horseradish, and lemon juice in the bowl of a food processor fitted with the steel blade. Process until the mixture is puréed. Or mash the trout to a paste and add the cream, horseradish, and lemon juice. Split the profiteroles and carefully remove any moist dough with the tip of a spoon. Spoon the filling into a pastry bag fitted with a small plain nozzle and pipe in the filling, or spoon the filling directly into the bottoms of the profiteroles, heaping it slightly, and replace the tops. (Leftover filling may be used as a sandwich or canapé spread.) Place the profiteroles on a dish and serve.

Profiteroles with Pâté Filling

24 profiteroles

6	ounces soft liver pâté or *pâté de foie gras*	24	baked Profiteroles (see Volume 4 Index)
3	tablespoons Madeira		

In a mixing bowl, beat the pâté and Madeira until smooth and well blended. Split the profiteroles, carefully scrape out any moist dough with the tip of a spoon, spoon the filling into a pastry bag fitted with a small plain nozzle and pipe into the profiteroles. Or spoon the filling directly into the bottoms, heaping it slightly, and then replace the tops. (Leftover filling may be used as a sandwich or canapé spread.) Place the profiteroles on a dish and serve.

Profiteroles with Ham and Chutney Filling

24 profiteroles

6	ounces boiled ham	24	baked Profiteroles (see
1½	tablespoons fruit chutney		Volume 4 Index)
1½	tablespoons dairy sour cream		

Mince the ham, either by hand or in a food processor fitted with the steel blade. Place the ham in a mixing bowl. Mince the fruit in the chutney. Add the chutney and sour cream to the ham and mix until well blended. Split the profiteroles, carefully scrape out any moist dough with the tip of a spoon, spoon the filling into the bottom of each one, heaping it slightly, and then replace the tops. (Leftover filling may be used for sandwiches or canapés.) Place the profiteroles on a dish and serve.

Profiteroles with Shrimp Filling

24 profiteroles

2	medium-size scallions		salt
6	ounces cooked shrimps		freshly ground black pepper
3	tablespoons dairy sour cream	24	baked Profiteroles (see
	pinch of ground mace		Volume 4 Index)

Wash scallions, trim and chop fine. Shell the shrimps, devein them if you wish, and place in the bowl of a food processor fitted with the steel blade. Add the sour cream and mace and process until the mixture is puréed. Add the chopped scallions and process briefly. Or chop the shrimps almost to a paste and combine with the sour cream, scallions and mace. Add salt and pepper to taste. Split the profiteroles, carefully scrape out any moist dough with the tip of a spoon, spoon the puréed shrimps into the bottom, heaping it slightly, and replace the tops. (Leftover filling may be used as a sandwich or canapé spread.) Arrange the profiteroles on a dish and serve.

Profiteroles with Ham and Asparagus Filling

24 profiteroles

½ teaspoon salt
6 asparagus tips, about 1½ inches long
4 ounces boiled ham
4 tablespoons dairy sour cream

freshly grated nutmeg
salt
freshly ground black pepper
24 baked Profiteroles (see Volume 4 Index)

In a saucepan, bring 1 quart water to a boil, add the salt and asparagus tips, and simmer until the asparagus is barely tender, 3 to 8 minutes, depending on size. Drain the tips and refresh under cold running water. Drain again and pat dry. Cut the tips into ¼-inch dice and place in a mixing bowl. Chop the ham fine, either by hand or in a food processor fitted with the steel blade. Add the ham, sour cream, and nutmeg to the asparagus and stir gently until well combined, taking care not to mash the asparagus. Season with salt and pepper to taste. Split the profiteroles, carefully scrape out any moist dough with the tip of a spoon, fill the bottoms with the ham and asparagus mixture, heaping it slightly, and replace the tops. (Leftover filling may be used for sandwiches or canapés.) Arrange the profiteroles on a dish and serve.

Profiteroles with Smoked Salmon Filling

24 profiteroles

6 ounces smoked salmon
1 lemon
3 tablespoons dairy sour cream

freshly ground black pepper
24 baked Profiteroles (see Volume 4 Index)

Cut the salmon into 1-inch pieces and place in the bowl of a food processor fitted with the steel blade. Juice the lemon to measure 1½ teaspoons. Add the sour cream, lemon juice and a few grindings of black pepper to the processor, then process until the salmon is puréed. Or chop the salmon almost to a paste and combine with the sour cream, lemon juice and black pepper. Split the profiteroles and carefully remove any moist dough with the tip of a spoon. Spoon the filling into a pastry bag fitted with a small plain nozzle and pipe it into the profiteroles. Or spoon the filling directly into the bottoms, heaping it slightly, and then replace the tops. (Leftover filling may be used as a sandwich or canapé spread.) Place the profiteroles on a dish and serve.

Lobster Newburg Bouchées

24 bouchées

7 ounces cooked lobster meat
1 shallot
2 teaspoons butter
4 teaspoons brandy
2 eggs

⅞ to 1 cup light cream
⅛ teaspoon salt
fresh-ground white pepper
24 baked 1½-inch Bouchée cases (see Volume 5 Index)

Preheat the oven to 425°F. Cut the lobster into ¼-inch dice and set aside. Peel and mince the shallot. Melt the butter in a skillet. Add the shallot and sauté over medium heat for 3 to 4 minutes, stirring often, until soft but not brown. Stir in the lobster and cook 2 to 3 minutes, stirring occasionally, until the lobster is hot. Warm the brandy in a small saucepan or in a metal ladle held over the heat. Carefully ignite it and immediately pour it over the lobster. Remove the pan from the heat and allow the flames to die out.

Separate the eggs, reserving the whites for another purpose. In a small bowl, beat the light cream and egg yolks together with a fork, then pour over the lobster mixture, stirring rapidly to prevent the heat remaining in the lobster pan from cooking the egg yolks. Add the salt and 3 grindings of pepper. Return the pan to low heat and cook, stirring constantly, until the mixture is thick. Cover loosely and keep the filling warm while you prepare the bouchée cases.

With the point of a sharp knife, lift out the small pastry lid in the center of each bouchée, then scrape out any moist pastry with the knife or a teaspoon. Place the cases on a baking sheet and spoon in the filling. (Leftover filling may be used as a topping for baked potatoes or served over hot biscuits or toast.) Replace the bouchée lids and bake the bouchées for about 10 minutes, or until heated through. Serve at once.

Seafood Bouchées

24 bouchées

¾	pound mussels
½	cup white wine or water
½	medium-size onion
2	teaspoons unsalted butter
2	medium-size mushrooms
5	ounces cooked shrimps
⅞	cup Béchamel Sauce (see Volume 3 Index)

7	tablespoons heavy cream
	pinch of salt
3	to 4 grindings of white pepper
24	baked 1½-inch Bouchée cases (see Volume 5 Index)
2	tablespoons minced parsley

To make the filling, scrub the mussels well under cold running water with a hard brush and pull or cut off their beards. Discard any mussels that are open. Leave mussels to soak in a bowl of cold water for 1 hour, then drain and rinse them again.

Preheat the oven to 425°F.

Bring the wine or water to a boil in a medium-size saucepan over medium heat. Add the mussels, cover the pan, and steam for 5 minutes, or until the mussels have opened. Lift them out with a slotted spoon. Scoop the mussels out of their shells and then coarsely chop. Place the mussels in a bowl and set aside. Discard the shells and reserve the mussel liquor for another purpose.

Peel the onion and chop fine. Melt the butter in a small heavy saucepan and add the chopped onion. Cook over low heat, stirring occasionally, for 4 to 5 minutes. While the onions are cooking, trim the mushroom stems and wipe the mushrooms with a damp cloth or paper towel. Chop the mushrooms. Shell the shrimps, devein them if you wish, and coarsely chop them.

Add the chopped mushrooms to the onions and cook for 5 minutes more. Remove the pan from the heat.

Put the béchamel sauce in a medium-size saucepan and stir in the onions and mushrooms. Add the mussels and shrimps and stir in the cream. Add the salt and pepper. Taste the mixture and add more seasoning if necessary.

To prepare the bouchée cases for filling, lift out their small pastry lids with the point of a sharp knife, and set aside. Scoop out any moist pastry with the knife point or a teaspoon. Place the bouchée cases on a baking sheet and spoon the filling into them. Fill the cases almost to overflowing. (Leftover filling may be used as topping for baked potatoes or served over hot biscuits.) Replace the bouchée lids. Set the bouchées in the oven for 10 minutes, or until they are heated through. Serve at once, garnished with a sprinkling of parsley.

Part Two

BRAISING AND STEWING GAME BIRDS, RABBIT, AND POULTRY

Alice B. Toklas tells a charming anecdote about a crate containing six white pigeons that were sent by a friend from the country. The pigeons were a welcome gift for it was wartime and food was scarce. The only problem, but it was a big one, was that the pigeons were very much alive and active: "Six white pigeons to be smothered, to be plucked, to be cleaned and all this to be accomplished before Gertrude Stein returned for she didn't like to see work being done." (*The Alice B. Toklas Cook Book*) Most cooks today would find themselves similarly perplexed if food were delivered to them in its live form. We have become quite accustomed to the services of the butcher, and our thank yous may be tinged with despair when a hunter presents us with a gift of wild birds.

Our forefathers relied heavily on game when they arrived on the shores of the New World. Many of them had come from countries in Europe where hunting and eating game was reserved for the aristocracy. Poaching of any sort was often punishable by death. It is easy to imagine their delight at the extraordinary abundance of wildlife that they found in the fields and forests of their new home. Extraordinary as well is the speed and efficiency with which many birds and beasts were hunted down to the point of extinction.

Although a good deal of sport hunting takes place today, game dishes of any sort are unknown on many tables. Not that we need to take gun or bow in hand to bag our own game dinners. A fair number of butchers and even the meat departments of some supermarkets carry a selection of game birds and rabbits. Some of what's available will be frozen and some will be from game farms and have a somewhat milder taste than bagged game.

The following is a round-up of information, some pertinent, some merely interesting, about the most common types of small game.

Partridge: Of the true partridges, there are many genera found throughout the Old World, but only one, the Chukar, has been successfully introduced here. It was brought from France in about 1660.

The European quail: Not native to this country either, though early settlers, encountering a similar bird, in the North called it quail, and in parts of the South called it partridge. To further confuse matters, the very same bird is widely known as the bobwhite. Thus the bobwhite is really the American quail, which is not really a quail at all. Quails, Old World and New, are reluctant fliers, which in part explains why they are so delicately fleshed and flavored. Dark meat, strongly flavored and generally tough, is made so by the abundance of blood vessels necessary to sustain flight.

Pheasant: Noblest of the game birds, named for Phasis, a river now called Rion in Soviet Georgia. It is from here that Jason and the Argonauts were said to have brought the first pheasant back to Greece when they returned from the land of Colchis and their quest for the golden fleece. The quail was remarked by Marco Polo and has been common for millennia in India as well as the Far East. Thomas Jefferson was interested in introducing it to America, but it is not known whether he was successful. There is evidence to indicate, however, that it was widely known here by the middle of the nineteenth century. Whatever its date of introduction, it is one of the most successfully imported game birds, well established and widely hunted in thirty-four states.

Squab: This is a pigeon less than four weeks old. Older pigeons are almost never served since the flesh of the mature bird gets quite tough. Though there are many varieties of pigeons and doves, including the unappetizing-looking city pigeon that is so fond of befouling park statuary, the common domesticated pigeon (and the most common source of squab) is thought to have been bred from the rock dove.

Hares and Rabbits: These familiar creatures had been known and eaten in both the New and Old Worlds long before the voyages of Columbus. Rather lean, white and delicately fleshed, these animals are enjoyed almost as variously as chicken, to which their taste is often compared. The distinction between hares and rabbits is subtle for anyone but a taxonomist or the most ardent collector of trivial information. There is also much confusion because of regional preferences in names. Grouped together as Lagomorphs, rabbits technically belong to the genus Cryctolagus, while hares belong to the genus Lepus. Of these remarkably similar animals, the hare is slightly larger, it does not burrow as the rabbit does, its young are born with their eyes open, and its heartbeat at rest (64 per minute) is roughly a third of the rabbit's. On a more practical level, the hare has never been successfully bred in captivity, whereas the reproductive impulses of the rabbit are notoriously irrepressible. Thus all hares are wild, while rabbit may be wild or domestic. Wild hares and wild rabbits taste quite similar; the domesticated rabbit is less gamy than either.

The confusion between the two animals is compounded by a mildly persistent piece of ancient snobbery: For some reason rabbit was considered a backwoods dish, or at least "low rent," while hare was considered a gourmet treasure of the game bag. Most experts agree the distinction is rubbish.

Though braising and stewing are fine methods for cooking poultry—as the tasty recipes included here demonstrate—they are the best methods for preparing game, which needs moist heat cooking to tenderize its tougher flesh and make it into succulent and delicious eating.

BRAISING, POT-ROASTING, STEWING

As poultry and game get older, they become tougher, making them unsuitable for roasting. However, they are often more flavorful at this stage. Using moist heat—braising, pot-roasting, stewing and cooking in casseroles—you can turn these older birds into delicious meals. These methods are just as useful for tender poultry when you want flavorful results with juicy texture and a sauce ready at the same time as the meat.

All wild game is less tender than domestic poultry, since it is running or flying freely and developing tougher muscles and ligaments. Therefore moist-heat methods are the best to use for most kinds of game birds and wild rabbit or hare. Even if you have bagged or purchased tender young game birds, the legs will require more cooking than the breast portion. In roasting game, the legs, wings, backs and necks are often set aside for stock making. In moist-heat cooking, these portions can be added to a stew or casserole to give more meat and good flavor.

All kinds of poultry can be braised or pot-roasted, and of course all make delicious casseroles and stews. Turkey parts, which can be tough, and older chickens are helped by these methods, but even small squabs and Rock Cornish game birds are successful prepared this way. Moist heat is an excellent cooking method for partridges, pheasants, quails, rabbit and hare. Wild duck and wild goose need special care because their natural diet can give their flesh a somewhat fishy taste.

Determining the Age of Poultry and Game

Domestic poultry is generally sold when young and rather small. If a chicken is more than 5 pounds, it is usually older and less tender, but it will be more flavorful than a young fryer. Ducks more than 5 pounds and geese more than 8 pounds may be less tender. Since most of our domestic ducks and geese are sold frozen, it is difficult to determine anything in advance except by using the weight as a guide. Be sure to purchase these frozen birds from a reliable supplier, and plan to use a moist-heat method for any that are very large. Cornish game birds and squabs are always young and can be counted on to be tender.

With game birds it is fairly easy to detect the age. In older birds the feathers under the wings will be fully formed rather than downy, cock pheasants will have pronounced spurs, and the scales on the legs and feet of birds will be larger and coarser than those of young specimens. The feet, beak and breastbone of older birds are rigid rather than

Separating Cooked Game Birds into Portions

| 1 | Transfer the cooked bird to a carving board or a flat platter. |

| 2 | Using kitchen scissors or poultry shears, cut away and discard the backbone of the bird. |

| 3 | Use a sharp knife to divide small birds into halves by cutting down the breastbone. |

pliable, and in old partridges the legs are red rather than yellow. If you are buying the birds already dressed, you can only take the butcher's word for their age, but it is worth knowing that most often birds sold toward the end of the game season will be beyond the age when they can be roasted successfully.

It is hard to judge the age of wild pigeons; they are almost always better braised or cooked in a casserole.

For judging the age of a rabbit, the only guideline is the ears. If the ears are soft and will tear easily, the animal is young. If they are tough, the animal is old. With cut-up rabbit it is impossible to judge age, so it is always best to play safe and braise, pot-roast, cook in a casserole or stew.

How Much to Buy

Allow 1 squab and 1 Rock Cornish game bird per person; each of these weighs about 1 pound. Nowadays larger Rock Cornish birds are being marketed; if the bird you buy weighs 1¼ to 2 pounds or more, it can easily make 2

4 Cut larger birds again into halves, cutting at the point where the leg joins the body.

portions. A chicken of 3 pounds will make 4 portions, 4 pounds will make 6 portions, and larger birds can be divided to serve 8 or more. A 5-pound duck cooked by moist heat usually provides 4 portions, but remember the old saying that a duck is too much for 2 and not enough for 4. An 8-pound goose will provide 6 to 8 portions, with some leftovers.

Quails are so tiny that at least 2 are needed for a single portion, and even that will not be a lot to eat. Partridges are generally bagged or sold at about 1 pound, and when braised or pot-roasted each makes 1 portion. However, when cooked with other ingredients as in a *chartreuse,* a single partridge can make 2 portions. A dressed pheasant of 3 to 3 ½ pounds will make 4 portions, although smaller, younger birds seldom serve more than 2. Wild ducks and geese will provide less edible meat than the same domestic birds since some portions will be too tough to serve and will be useful only for game stock.

Wild rabbits vary in size; allow at least ½ pound of dressed rabbit per portion; a 5-pound rabbit will provide 6 to 8 portions. Frozen rabbit is available in most markets in the United States. These are packed cut up, ½ rabbit to a package, weighing about 2¼ pounds. This amount of domestic rabbit will easily make 4 to 6 portions. There is considerably more meat in 2¼ pounds of rabbit than in the same weight of chicken. Hare, which is larger, will vary according to the individual catch. Allow ½ to ¾ pound of dressed hare for each portion.

Larding and Barding

Classical French recipes often direct the cook to wrap poultry or game in sheets of pork fat for braising, and many other recipes assume that the cook will lard any game. While lean game birds are often barded (wrapped in sheets of fat) for roasting, it is better not to add extra fat to braises or pot-roasts. Especially in braising, whatever goes into the pot is part of the finished dish, and extra fat is not desirable. The

taste of the pork fat may spoil the flavor of the dish.

A small amount of fat is used to brown the poultry or game, and for game some extra fat may be added—a few strips of bacon cut into small dice or arranged over the breasts of the birds.

Marinating

Naturally tender domestic poultry seldom needs marinating for tenderness, but a marinade can add flavor to otherwise bland chicken or turkey. All game tends to be dry, and the dryness increases as a game bird gets older. A marinade helps to break down tough fibers and moisturize the meat. Like marinades for meat, marinades for poultry and game are made with an acid to break down fibers, and oil to moisturize the flesh and carry the flavors of herbs and seasonings into the tissues. There are cooked and uncooked marinades for game.

When a pungent flavor is desired, a cooked marinade is used since cooking intensifies the flavor of the spices in the mixture. The ingredients are simmered for 30 minutes to 1 hour, then cooled to room temperature. Do not pour a hot marinade onto raw game for that would seal the outer surface and thus prevent the penetration of the marinade into the fibers; there would be little or no tenderizing or flavoring.

For an uncooked marinade, the ingredients are simply mixed together and poured over the meat.

For both kinds, crush the spices or berries and crumble any dried herb so that they will release their flavors. Because of the association of some flavors such as juniper berries with game, particularly venison, the use of a marinade flavored with this spice will give domestic meats a flavor that most people consider gamy.

Small birds may be adequately flavored in 1 hour, but larger game should be marinated at room temperature for at least 4 hours. The game should be turned from time to time so that all sides are moistened.

Rabbit Goulash

6 to 8 portions

1 rabbit, about 5 pounds fresh, 4½ pounds frozen, defrosted
6 medium-size onions
6 medium-size carrots
4 celery ribs
2 garlic cloves
2 tablespoons tomato purée
2 cups canned peeled plum tomatoes with their juices
4 teaspoons chopped fresh basil
2 bay leaves
salt
fresh-ground black pepper
1 cup dry white wine
2 teaspoons paprika
parsley sprigs

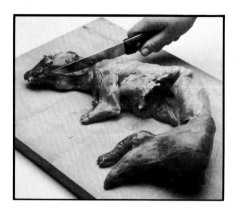

1 Cut off and discard the head and feet of the fresh rabbit.

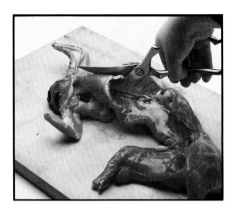

2 Cut through the breastbone from the belly opening to the neck.

3 Cut off the hind legs.

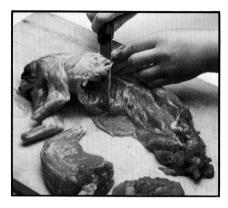

4 Cut off the front legs and upper part of the body. This is the forequarter.

5 Split the forequarter into halves down the center.

6 Cut remaining body into serving portions.

7 Peel and slice the onions. Scrape and slice carrots. Wash and chop celery. Peel and crush garlic.

8 Put rabbit pieces in a heavy 2½-quart casserole. Add vegetables, tomato pureé, canned tomatoes, garlic and herbs. Season.

9 Add wine and paprika. Cover, bring slowly to a boil, reduce heat, and simmer for 2 hours, until rabbit is tender. Transfer rabbit to platter.

10 Reduce sauce by boiling rapidly, uncovered, for 4 to 5 minutes. Pour sauce and vegetables over rabbit. Serve garnished with parsley sprigs.

Uncooked marinades can be strained and added to the liquid used for braising or for a sauce. Cooked marinades are best discarded after use, as the pungency of the concentrated spice tastes may overwhelm the flavor of any sauce.

Preparing Poultry and Game

Be sure the poultry or game bird is completely dressed—plucked of all feathers and with all the viscera removed. Gizzards, neck and wing tips can be used for stock; if you have only a few, freeze them and save until you have enough to use. The livers, not good for stock, can be used in pâté.

Small birds, such as squabs, quails and Rock Cornish game birds, can be braised or pot-roasted whole. The dish will be enhanced if accompanying vegetables are cooked with the birds; since these birds will be cooked relatively quickly, the vegetables will not be overcooked. Larger birds—chickens, ducks, turkey and most large game birds—will be more evenly cooked if they are quartered or cut into smaller pieces. The leg and thigh portions can be cooked for a longer time to become tender. The wings of some game birds may also need a few extra minutes to become tender.

If your bird is young and seems to be tender, plan to cook it whole; whole birds retain maximum juice and flavor. The birds can be cut into portions afterward (see Separating Cooked Game Birds into Portions). Wash the bird thoroughly inside and out with cold running water. Season the cavity with salt and pepper. If you like, an onion, a celery rib, a parsley sprig and a bay leaf can be stuffed into the cavity. Truss the bird.

Rabbit and hare are usually purchased already cut into sections. If you have a whole rabbit, see the directions for Rabbit Goulash for steps in cutting a rabbit into portions. Rabbit and hare are so long that they will always need to be sectioned for braising or pot-roasting.

Braising and Pot-Roasting

The chief difference between these two methods is the amount of liquid used. In braising, usually very little liquid is added; often the moisture is supplied by the vegetables and the poultry or game itself. In both processes the bird is first browned in hot fat, which may be a mixture of oil and butter, or bacon fat for game.

For successful braising the pot should hold the pieces or the whole bird snugly so that the juices are mixed with the *fonds de braise,* a mixture of flavoring vegetables with pork rind or bits of bacon. Bacon strips are often added to lean game as well. (See Volume 4 Index for more about the *fonds de braise.*) The usual vegetables are onion, carrot and celery, but for game, turnips and some fruits such as apples and quinces may be added. For rabbit, prunes are a good addition.

For pot-roasting, the browned meat is seasoned and put in a suitable heavy pot; the liquid is added and brought quickly to a boil. The heat is reduced to a simmer and often the cooking is done in the oven. Instead of resting on a bed of vegetables, the meat is frequently placed on a shallow rack so that the bottom does not brown too much during cooking. Any vegetables to be added to a pot-roast are added toward the end, just long enough to become tender.

Braises and pot-roasts can be cooked on top of the stove or in the oven. The casserole or pot used should be heavy, with a tight-fitting lid.

Casseroles and Stews

Poultry and game birds are made into casseroles and stews following the same procedure used for meats (see Volume 4 Index). Birds are cut into sections rather than into smaller cubes, and the bones are retained for more flavor. All the ingredients added to the casserole or stewpot are part of the finished dish, with the exception of a *bouquet garni.* Long slow cooking is the rule for both preparations.

For brown stews or casseroles, the pieces of poultry or game are rolled in seasoned flour, or shaken in a bag of flour, and then browned in a small amount of fat. To add color, paprika can be added to the flour; to add flavor, crumbled dried herbs can be added. The browning can be done in the casserole or stewpot, but it is often easier to do it in a skillet, working with a few pieces at a time to prevent steaming. This method also eliminates excess fat in the final dish. For domesticated poultry, the proper fat is a mixture of oil and butter, from 1 to 3 tablespoons per pound of meat; for game birds bacon fat is sometimes preferred for added flavor.

In white stews, the poultry or game is not browned first. These stews are known as fricassees and blanquettes. In a fricassee, a favorite chicken stew, the poultry is quickly sautéed in butter to seal the outer surface, but it is not browned. After sautéing the pieces can be rolled in flour. The liquid is added and the stew is simmered until the chicken is tender. The flour coating on the pieces will thicken the liquid. A blanquette is made of white meats started in cold liquid and gently simmered until tender. In this case the meat is neither browned nor sautéed. The liquid that results is a velouté, a white sauce based on stock rather than milk.

To finish these white stews, a liaison of egg yolk and cream (1 egg yolk and 3 tablespoons heavy cream) is sometimes used to enrich and thicken the velouté. Some stews use only an egg yolk. Beat the liaison to mix, then stir in several tablespoons of the hot liquid to warm the mixture. Turn the liaison into the stew, stirring all the while. Sauces that contain both flour and egg yolk must be brought to the boiling point, then removed from heat. Do not let the sauce boil after adding the liaison lest the cream curdle and the whole mixture separate.

The amount of liquid used in a stew or casserole should be in proportion to the amount of poultry or game. Add 1 cup liquid for 1 pound meat, or less if the vegetables used have a high

Coq au Vin *(Chicken in Wine)*

While chicken and other white meats are usually paired with white wine, this French classic uses red wine, which gives a rich sauce and excellent flavor to the dish. The wine should be of good quality, and it is usual to serve the same kind of wine to drink with the dish.

This dish is said to have originated in the province of Auvergne, but today it is made in all the wine-producing areas, where the name is changed from just *vin* to reflect the specific wine.

Once the bird used was a cock or cockerel, naturally less tender than a pullet; the braising method was a good choice for tenderizing the bird. The tender chickens available today become deliciously flavorful with this method.

The traditional garnishes are tiny onions, button mushrooms, little pieces of bacon and crisply fried bread triangles. Decorate the bread triangles by dipping one corner first into softened butter, then into minced parsley.

6 portions

1	roasting chicken, 4 to 5 pounds	1	sprig of fresh thyme, or 1 teaspoon crumbled dried thyme	6	tablespoons butter
2	teaspoons tomato purée			6	tablespoons brandy
1	chicken bouillon cube	1	cup robust red wine	12	ounces small button mushrooms
1	small yellow onion	6	ounces sliced bacon		
	salt	24	small white onions (silverskins)	2	tablespoons flour
	fresh-ground black pepper			12	triangles of white bread
1	large garlic clove	4	tablespoons olive oil	4	tablespoons minced fresh parsley
1	bay leaf				

Coq au Vin (continued)

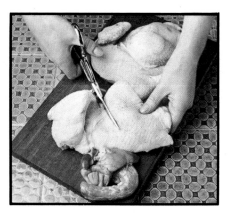

1 Wash chicken and giblets in cold water. Drain. Quarter chicken, cover, and refrigerate.

2 Cover giblets and trimmings with water. Add the tomato purée and the bouillon cube.

3 Peel and slice yellow onion and add to giblets. Season. Simmer for 30 minutes. Strain and reserve the stock.

7 Heat 2 tablespoons of the oil and 2 tablespoons of the butter in a skillet. Brown bacon and onions for 5 minutes. Remove to plate.

8 Starting skin side down, brown chicken in the skillet, turning until evenly golden on all sides.

9 Transfer chicken to a flameproof casserole. Flame with warmed brandy. Add onions and lardoons.

13 Transfer mushrooms, onions and lardoons to the platter. Keep chicken and garnishes hot.

14 There should be about ¾ cup sauce. Concentrate it, if necessary, by boiling to reduce. Season the sauce.

15 Skim surplus fat from sauce. Knead flour and 2 tablespoons butter together in a small bowl to make beurre manié.

4 Peel and slice garlic and put in a saucepan with the bay leaf, thyme and red wine.

5 Simmer wine over medium heat, uncovered, for about 15 minutes, until reduced by half.

6 Trim any rind from bacon and slice into 1-inch strips, ¼ inch thick. Peel the small white onions.

10 Strain wine over chicken. Add the stock, cover, and simmer chicken for 40 minutes.

11 Wipe mushrooms with damp cloth or paper towels and trim base of stems. Add mushrooms to chicken and simmer for 5 minutes.

12 Transfer chicken pieces to a warmed serving platter.

16 Over low heat whisk the beurre manié, piece by piece, into the sauce. Simmer for a few minutes.

17 While the sauce simmers, sauté the bread triangles in remaining oil and butter over medium heat.

18 Pour the thickened, glossy sauce over the chicken and garnish with bread triangles dipped into parsley.

moisture content. White stock, wine and water are the most frequently used, but beer, cider, orange or other fruit juice, and tomato paste for color, are all used occasionally. Sweet cream and dairy sour cream are also used, but they must be added just before serving because long cooking causes them to separate.

The most common additional ingredients are onions, carrots, parsnips, leeks, celery and zucchini. Tomatoes and peppers can be used for stews with a Provençal or Spanish accent. Dried beans can help to turn a little meat into an inexpensive and nourishing meal. There are also less usual recipes that include fruits such as pineapple, apricots, oranges or dried fruits.

Herbs, paprika, mustard, curry powder and chili powder give a dish an unusual flavor.

Equipment

The best cooking pot for braises, pot-roasts, stews and casseroles is a covered flameproof dish attractive enough to take to the table. If desired, the meat can be browned in it on top of the stove, then transferred to the oven for slow simmering, and served from the same dish. If your casserole is not flameproof, use it for oven cooking and brown the meat in a skillet. If you do this, be sure to deglaze the skillet after the browning is finished because the browned bits in the skillet will add color and flavor.

If the stew is simmered on top of the stove, a heavy stewpot can be used for all the steps. Make sure the lid is tight-fitting, otherwise liquid will evaporate, carrying a lot of flavor with it. If the cover does not fit well, or if you lack a cover, place a piece of aluminum foil over the stew, pressing it close to the surface of the ingredients to keep all the moisture and flavor inside.

Adding Vegetables and Liquid

When the meat for a stew or casserole has been browned and transferred to a plate or to the baking dish, the flavoring vegetables are often browned. Reduce the heat under the browning pan to moderate and sauté sliced or chopped onions in the fat remaining in the pan. Garlic can also be added at this stage. The slow browning of onions until they are slightly caramelized adds color and flavor to a brown stew. Sometimes sugar is added to the onions and caramelized in the same way. Some recipes call for browning root vegetables also; others add them halfway through the cooking so they retain their texture and do not become too soft.

When onions are golden brown, remove the pan from heat and stir in the flour. Set the pan over low heat and stir and cook the roux to the desired color. For a brown stew, this should be nut brown without being burned. For a white stew the onions are only lightly sautéed, or sweated, and the roux is stirred long enough for the fat and flour to blend before the liquid is added. The onions must be left in the pan when making the roux because they will have absorbed a good deal of the fat.

Remove the pan from heat and add the liquid, stirring constantly. Return to heat and cook gently until flour and liquid have thickened into a smooth sauce. This blending is easier if the liquid is hot or warm when added. Bring the sauce to the boiling point. Remove pan from heat again, return the browned meat to the sauce, and add herbs and seasonings. If you are using a separate pan for the browning and sauce, transfer the meat and sauce to the oven dish. Cover the dish and place it on a rack in the center of the heated oven, or simmer on top of the stove. Additional vegetables can be added halfway through.

At the end of cooking, if there is a layer of liquid fat floating on top of the stew or casserole, remove it with a skimmer or absorb it with paper towels.

Thickening the Sauce of a Braise or Stew

The most flavorful sauce for a braise is made by reducing the liquid, which will concentrate all the flavors. Strain the liquid into a clean saucepan and boil it rapidly to reduce it until you have the amount needed, or until the sauce is as thick as you like it. It will be only moderately thick, but the flavor will be good, uncomplicated by other additions.

Another method is to purée the liquid with the vegetables from the *fonds de braise*; the puréed vegetables will serve to thicken the sauce.

In braises and stews where the meat has been tossed in flour before browning, or has been dusted with flour after browning, the sauce will usually be thick enough.

If no flour has been used, *beurre manié* (see page 34) can be added, a small piece at a time. Do this over low heat and keep stirring, as you add, to blend the butter and flour into the sauce without letting it become lumpy. Cook for 2 or 3 minutes, until the sauce is thick.

The addition of cream, sweet or sour, can also help to thicken a sauce. Be sure to do that at the very end and leave the sauce over heat only long enough to warm the mixture.

Timing and Temperature

When poultry and game are done the joints should not show any pink and the juices should be colorless.

All casseroles and stews are best cooked at 325° to 350°F. They should be simmering, so turn down the heat if necessary, or turn it up if the contents do not seem to be cooking at all. It is practical to bring the liquid to a boil before turning the heat to simmering temperature, because you can be sure the cooking is well started. After this, low heat is needed for all moist-heat methods. The liquid, whether a small amount as in braising or a larger amount as in a stew, must never be maintained at a boil for this shrinks the meat fibers and causes them to release juices. The liquid that results will be flavorful but the meat will be tough and may be stringy.

When vegetables are added partway through, you may need to increase the temperature briefly to bring the contents of the casserole back to the simmering point. The addition of cold vegetables causes the temperature to drop.

Domestic poultry is naturally tender, so you can count on quick cooking. When dealing with wild game, the following chart is a guide only. The best plan is to test for doneness with a thin skewer to see if the juices run clear and the meat feels tender. Test again if the game is not ready at first. Size is not always a good indication of age or tenderness. Remember that the legs of all birds will need to cook longer than the breast portions.

Separating Cooked Birds into Portions

After a bird has been cooked whole, transfer it to a carving board or a platter. Small birds such as squabs and Rock Cornish game birds can be served whole, but they are easier to eat if they have been halved. Partridge is always best halved. Using kitchen scissors or poultry shears, cut away the backbone. Using a sharp knife, cut through the breastbone. Arrange the birds cavity side down on a bed of vegetables or on any grain or on toast.

Larger birds can be cut into 4 portions. Halve as described, then cut again into halves, cutting at the point where the leg joins the body. Keep the portions warm in a low oven while finishing the sauce.

Cooking Ahead and Reheating

Poultry is always most tender and flavorful when served as soon as it is cooked, as reheating tends to dry it out and cause loss of flavor. Even when using moist-heat methods there is some flavor loss in reheating, but the poultry will still be tender and juicy. Choose a moist-heat method, therefore, if you are obliged to prepare the poultry or game ahead of time.

Moist-Heat Cooking at 325° to 350°F

(When cooking at the lower temperature, use the longer time)

	minutes per pound
chicken	15 to 20
turkey	20 to 25
duck (domestic)	20 to 25
goose (domestic)	20 to 25
quail	18 to 20 (total)
squab	45 to 60 (total)
Rock Cornish game bird	45 to 60 (total)
guinea hen	60 to 75 (total)
partridge	1½ to 2 hours (total)
pheasant	25 to 30
rabbit	25 to 35

If you are cooking a casserole or a stew for another day, do not add cream, either sweet or sour, to the portion to be stored, as the cream could curdle on reheating. Instead, add the cream to the stored portion after it has been heated to serving temperature.

Cooking with Beer, Wine and Spirits

There is no mystique about cooking with wine; in wine-growing areas it is a natural local ingredient used to round out the flavor of a dish (see page 35 of Volume 4 for more information about this).

While white wines are most usual with poultry, red is used for one of the most famous chicken stews, *coq au vin* (see Index), and red is a natural companion to many game birds. Red wine is not suitable for rabbit as it discolors the meat. Keep these considerations in mind also when choosing a marinade for poultry or game.

Fortified wines include sherry, Madeira, port, Marsala, and aperitif wines such as vermouth. Small amounts of these can add a special flavor to a casserole or stew.

Wine must be cooked sufficiently to evaporate the alcohol, thus removing the raw taste. The residual essences mellow and mingle with the other ingredients. When wine is used in casseroles, the alcohol evaporates naturally during the long slow cooking. Fast boiling will also evaporate the alcohol, reduce the volume of wine, and concentrate the flavor. To do this, pour the wine into a wide saucepan so that the maximum surface area is exposed. Boil rapidly, uncovered, until the wine is reduced by the required amount, usually by a third or a half. The concentrated flavor is useful in a dish that is cooked for a relatively short time, such as the *coq au vin*.

Beer is another choice for the liquid, and is frequently used for cooking, as is cider. In Great Britain cider has always been considered a natural alternative to white wine and has been used for cooking in the same way. British cider is slightly alcoholic and mildly bubbly, unlike American cider, but our cider adds good flavor to poultry and game stews. It is particularly good with duck and goose.

Spirits are used in small quantities for flavoring. They are also used for flaming game birds after browning. The burning alcohol consumes excess fat and degreases the food. The concentrated essences of the spirit, which are left behind after flaming, contribute a delicious taste to the dish. The spirits for flaming should have good flavor and high proof. Brandy is also a major ingredient in the marinade for game used here (see Index).

Game Stock

makes 6 to 8 cups

3	pounds neck bones, backbones, breastbones, wings and trimmings of game, all one kind or a mixture of game birds, rabbit, and/or hare	4	celery ribs	
		1	large leek	
		1	large onion	
		3	whole cloves	
		1	large bay leaf	
8	ounces carrots	4	peppercorns	

Put all the bones and trimmings in a large stockpot and cover with cold water. Bring slowly to a boil, skimming from time to time. Let the water boil for 5 minutes, then pour it off, dumping the bones into a large colander. Rinse bones and wash the stockpot. Return bones to the pot and add enough water to cover by 2 inches, at least 6 quarts. Wash the carrots, celery and leek, trim them, and cut into chunks. Peel the onion and stud with the cloves. Crumble the bay leaf and crack the peppercorns. Add all these ingredients to the pot and bring the water slowly to a boil. Reduce heat to a simmer and cook the stock for at least 3 hours, skimming the surface often.

Taste the stock; it should be flavorful; if not, let it simmer for another hour. Pour the stock and solids into a colander set over a large bowl. Let the liquid settle for about 10 minutes, then, ladling the stock through a sieve lined with several layers of moistened cheesecloth, turn it into a clean saucepan. Let it cool completely, then lift off any fat that has risen to the surface.

Variation: To have brown game stock, put the blanched bones and trimmings and all the vegetables in a large roasting pan and brown them well in a 400°F oven for at least 40 minutes. Turn the pieces halfway through the browning. Be sure to deglaze the roasting pan and add the bits and deglazing liquid to the stockpot. Combine browned ingredients, cloves, bay leaf, peppercorns and water, and proceed as in the basic recipe.

Red Wine Marinade for Game

This is a cooked marinade. It should be used when a pungent flavor is desired, since cooking intensifies the flavor of the spices. Because it is so strongly flavored, it is not advisable to use it again in the cooking or in any sauce. Use a red-wine marinade only for dark meats or game birds with dark flesh, since it discolors white meat. It is not suitable for rabbit.

makes 1 cup

1	medium-size onion	1	cup dry red wine
4	black peppercorns	4	tablespoons olive oil
4	juniper berries	1	cup water
2	bay leaves		

Peel and mince the onion. Crush peppercorns and juniper berries in a mortar; the finer the pieces, the stronger the flavor. Crumble the bay leaves. Put these ingredients in a saucepan and stir in the wine, oil and water. Bring the mixture to a boil and simmer for 30 minutes to 1 hour. Let the marinade cool to room temperature.

Pour the cooled marinade as is, or strained, over the game and let it sit in a cool place or in the refrigerator for at least 4 hours, overnight if possible. Turn the game from time to time so that all sides are moistened with the marinade. The longer the meat is marinated, the more sour it will be and the more the natural taste of the meat will be altered. It is possible to use this marinade on lamb and make it taste like game.

Brandy Marinade for Game

This is an uncooked marinade, suitable for all white meats. After marinating, this can be strained and used as part of the cooking liquid for braising or pot-roasting.

makes 1 cup

1 large onion	1 cup brandy
8 parsley stems	1 teaspoon crumbled dried thyme
4 allspice berries	4 tablespoons olive oil
2 bay leaves	

Peel and mince the onion. Chop the parsley stems and crush them slightly with the back of a spoon to release more flavor. Crush the allspice berries in a mortar, and crumble the bay leaves. Combine all the ingredients in a bowl with a pouring spout. Place the rabbit or game bird or poultry in a ceramic or glass container and pour the marinade over the meat. Turn the pieces over to moisten all sides. Marinate the meat in a cool place or in the refrigerator for 1 to 4 hours, depending on the size of the pieces. Small portions need only brief marinating—30 minutes to 1 hour. This uncooked marinade serves to flavor rather than to tenderize.

Chartreuse de Perdreaux
(Partridges Cooked with Cabbage)

This is a simplified version of a classic French dish, named for the Chartreuse, a Carthusian monastery. The dish was originally made with vegetables only and was molded.

8 portions

4	partridges, 1¼ pounds each
2	large Savoy cabbages, 1½ pounds each
6	ounces lean bacon
2	small onions
2	carrots
6	tablespoons butter
8	ounces pork sausages

1	Bouquet Garni (see Volume 1 Index)
1½	teaspoons salt
½	teaspoon fresh-ground black pepper
5	cups Game Stock (see Index) or Chicken Stock (see Volume 1 Index) or canned broth

Have the partridges dressed and prepared for cooking. Truss them. Trim the cabbages, discard any coarse outer leaves, wash the cabbages, and shred them by hand or in a food processor fitted with the shredding disk. Dice the bacon. Peel and slice the onions. Scrub, scrape, and slice the carrots. Preheat oven to 325°F.

Place the shredded cabbage and diced bacon in a large saucepan half filled with water. Set the pan over high heat and bring water to a boil. Boil the cabbage, uncovered, for 5 minutes, stirring occasionally, until the color is bright green. Drain cabbage and bacon in a large colander and rinse with cold water. Do this in batches if the colander is small.

Melt the butter in a large skillet over moderate heat. Add the partridges, 2 at a time. Reduce heat to medium low and brown the birds for 10 minutes, turning them frequently to brown all sides. Using tongs or 2 large spoons, transfer birds to a plate. Brown remaining birds in the same way and transfer to a plate. Add the onions and carrots to the skillet. Increase heat to medium and sauté them, stirring occasionally, for 5 to 7 minutes, until onions are soft and translucent but not browned. Use a slotted spoon to transfer the vegetables to a plate. Add the sausages to the skillet and fry them for 3 minutes, turning them frequently to brown them on all sides. Remove pan from heat and set aside.

Place half of the cabbage and bacon in an ovenproof 3-quart casserole. Sprinkle onions and carrots over the cabbage and place the partridges on top. Add the *bouquet garni* and sprinkle salt and pepper over all. Arrange the sausages around the sides of the casserole and top with remaining cabbage and bacon. Pour in the stock and cover the casserole. Braise the partridges in the oven for 1½ hours, until they are tender.

Remove casserole from oven, discard the *bouquet garni,* and spoon the top layer of cabbage and bacon onto a warmed large serving platter. Keep warm. Remove partridges to a carving board, discard the trussing strings, and halve them, discarding the backbones. Place the birds, cavity sides down, on the cabbage. Garnish with the carrots and onions and place the rest of the cabbage around the birds. Cut the sausages into thick slices and arrange them around the platter. Pour a little of the cooking liquid over the partridges to moisten them.

Note: Any remaining cooking liquid can be reserved for other uses. Any remaining cabbage can be served for second helpings or can be reserved for another meal. This recipe works well for guinea hens, pheasants and lean ducks.

Partridges with White Wine and Vegetables

4 portions

4	partridges
1	teaspoon salt
½	teaspoon fresh-ground black pepper
4	lean bacon strips
3	garlic cloves
12	small white onions
12	small new potatoes
6	small carrots

4	small zucchini, about 12 ounces altogether
4	tablespoons butter
1	lemon
1	Bouquet Garni (see Volume 1 Index)
½	cup dry white wine
1	cup water
¼	teaspoon grated nutmeg
½	cup shelled green peas

Have the partridges dressed and prepared for cooking. Sprinkle the cavities with half of the salt and half of the pepper. Truss the birds. Chop the bacon. Peel the garlic and put through a press. Peel the small onions, blanch them, and drain well. Scrub and scrape the new potatoes. Scrub and scrape the carrots and quarter them lengthwise. Wash and trim zucchini and cut them crosswise into ¼-inch slices.

Melt the butter in a large flameproof casserole over medium heat. Add the partridges and cook for 5 to 8 minutes, until they are lightly and evenly browned, turning them with tongs to brown all sides. While the birds are browning, grate the lemon rind to measure 2 teaspoons. Assemble the *bouquet garni,* using 4 parsley sprigs, 1 thyme sprig and 1 bay leaf. Use tongs to transfer the birds to a plate; keep them warm. Add the chopped bacon to the casserole. Increase heat to medium-high and sauté bacon for 5 minutes, until crisp and brown. Remove casserole from heat. Use a slotted spoon to remove the bacon pieces to paper towels to drain. Pour the fat out of the casserole.

Pour the wine and water into the casserole and return it to medium heat. Stir in the garlic, nutmeg and lemon rind and drop in the *bouquet garni.* Return partridges to the casserole and bring the liquid to a boil. Add the onions, potatoes and carrots and reduce heat to low. Simmer partridges and vegetables for 15 minutes. Add the peas, zucchini and cooked bacon and cook for 15 minutes longer, or until the partridges are done to your taste. If the vegetables are done and the birds need longer cooking, lift out the vegetables so they do not become mushy; return them at the end for reheating.

Remove and discard the *bouquet garni.* Snip and remove the trussing strings from the birds. Serve the partridges and vegetables from the casserole.

Pheasant Braised in Red Wine

4 portions

2	young pheasants	4	ounces mushrooms
1	teaspoon salt	1¾	cups dry red wine
½	teaspoon fresh-ground black pepper	1	bay leaf
2	medium-size onions	4	bacon strips
6	tablespoons butter	4	tablespoons beurre manié (see page 34)
1	tablespoon vegetable oil	½	cup heavy cream

Have the pheasants dressed and prepared for cooking. Rub the cavities of the birds with half of the salt and pepper. Peel and chop the onions. Put one quarter of the chopped onion into the cavity of each bird; set remaining onion aside. Truss the birds.

Melt the butter with the oil in a large skillet set over high heat. Add the pheasants and reduce heat to medium. Brown the birds on all sides for 6 to 8 minutes, turning them frequently. Transfer pheasants to a large flameproof casserole and keep hot. Add remaining onion to the skillet and cook, stirring occasionally, for 8 to 10 minutes, until onion is golden brown. While onion is cooking, wipe mushrooms with damp cloth or paper towels, trim base of stems, and cut caps and stems into thin slices. Pour the wine into the skillet. Increase heat to high and bring to a boil, stirring constantly. Add remaining salt and pepper, the bay leaf and the sliced mushrooms. Reduce heat to medium and cook the mixture for 5 minutes.

Place the bacon strips on the breasts of the pheasants and pour the wine mixture over them. Cover the casserole and set it over low heat. Braise for 50 minutes to 1 hour, until pheasants are tender. Discard the bacon. Transfer birds to a carving board or a platter, cover them with foil, and keep them warm while finishing the sauce.

Set the casserole over high heat and boil the liquid until reduced by half. Reduce heat to medium and add the *beurre manié,* a little at a time, stirring constantly. Use only enough of the *beurre manié* to thicken the sauce lightly; it should not be very thick or pasty. Cook for 2 or 3 minutes, until the sauce is smooth. Stir in the cream and continue cooking for 2 or 3 minutes. Do not let the sauce boil after adding the cream. Pour the sauce into a sauceboat and keep warm. Remove trussing strings, carve the pheasants, and serve them with the sauce.

Perdreaux en Cocotte Normande

(Partridges in the Style of Normandy)

2 portions

2	partridges
½	cup Brandy Marinade (see Index)
2	lean bacon strips
1	medium-size onion
3	cooking apples, preferably Rome Beauty
½	cup cider

½	cup Game Stock (see Index) or Chicken Stock (see Volume 1 Index) or canned broth
1	Bouquet Garni (see Volume 1 Index)
2	tablespoons butter
	salt
	fresh-ground black pepper
	parsley sprigs

Dress the partridges and prepare for cooking. Wash them inside and out, pat dry, and truss them. Place them in a ceramic or glass dish and pour the marinade over them. Marinate the birds for 4 hours or overnight in a cool place or in the refrigerator, turning them several times to moisten all sides.

Preheat oven to 350°F. Cut the bacon into small strips and place the pieces in a flameproof casserole large enough to hold the partridges. Cook the bacon over low heat until the fat is released. Add the partridges, raise heat to medium, and brown well on all sides. Transfer the birds to a plate. Peel and chop the onion and add to the fat in the casserole. Peel and chop one of the apples and add to the onion. Cook over low heat for about 3 minutes, turning from time to time. Return partridges to the casserole. Pour in the cider, stock and strained marinade. Add the *bouquet garni.* Cover the casse-role and place in the oven. Braise the partridges for 2 to 2½ hours, until they are tender when pierced with a skewer.

Just before the birds are done, peel, core and slice the remaining 2 apples into rings. Melt the butter in a heavy skillet over low heat and sauté the apple rings until golden on both sides. Set aside.

Remove partridges from the casserole. Halve the birds along the backbone and cut away the backbones. Place the birds on a warmed serving dish and arrange the apple rings around them. Keep the partridges warm in a low oven. Strain the liquid in the casserole into a clean saucepan. Boil rapidly for about 4 minutes, until reduced and slightly thickened. Check the seasoning and add additional seasoning if needed. Spoon a little of the hot sauce over the birds and serve the rest in a sauceboat alongside. Garnish the dish with parsley sprigs.

Braised Quails with Juniper

4 to 6 portions

12	quails
3	shallots
4	juniper berries
2	lemons
1	large orange
3	tablespoons olive oil
1	teaspoon salt

½	teaspoon fresh-ground white pepper
¼	cup dry Madeira wine
¼	cup Game Stock (see Index) or Chicken Stock (see Volume 1 Index) or canned broth

If quails are fresh, dress them and prepare them for cooking. If they are frozen, let them defrost in the refrigerator overnight. Peel and mince the shallots. Crush the juniper berries in a mortar. Grate the lemon rind to measure 3 tablespoons. Juice the orange to measure ¼ cup. Heat the oil in a flameproof casserole large enough to hold the quails. Brown the quails quickly, four at a time, until evenly colored all over. As each batch is browned, transfer quails to a plate. When the browning is completed, add chopped shallots to the casserole and sauté until golden. Return all the quails to the casserole and sprinkle them with salt, pepper, juniper berries and lemon rind. Pour in the orange juice, Madeira and stock. Turn the birds carefully in the liquid to moisten all sides. Cover the casserole and braise the quails for 15 to 20 minutes, until very tender. Serve the quails, 2 or 3 to a portion, on a bed of wild rice or hominy.

Pheasant with Celery and Cream

4 portions

2	pheasants	½	cup port wine
1	cup Brandy Marinade (see Index)	1	Bouquet Garni (see Volume 1 Index)
4	lean bacon strips	2	celery hearts
1	cup Game Stock (see Index) or Chicken Stock (see Volume 1 Index) or canned broth	1	large egg
		½	cup heavy cream
			salt
			fresh-ground black pepper

Have the pheasants dressed and prepared for cooking. Truss them, and place them in a ceramic or glass container just large enough to hold them. Pour the marinade over them and let them marinate at a cool temperature or in the refrigerator for at least 4 hours, or overnight if they are not young and tender. Turn the birds occasionally to moisten all sides. Remove the birds from the marinade and pat them dry. Strain any remaining marinade and set it aside.

Cut the bacon into small strips and fry them in a heavy flameproof casserole. Pour off all but 3 tablespoons fat. Preheat oven to 350°F. Brown the pheasants in the bacon fat until evenly colored on all sides. Pour in the stock, port wine and strained marinade. Add the *bouquet garni*. Cover the casserole. Place the casserole in the oven and braise the birds for about 30 minutes.

Meanwhile, wash and trim the celery hearts and cut them into thick rounds or quarter them lengthwise. After the first 30 minutes, add the celery to the casserole. Continue cooking for about 2 hours longer, until the legs of the birds are tender. Lift pheasant and celery out of the casserole. Using poultry shears, split the pheasants along the backbone and cut away the backbone. Divide each half again into 2 portions. Arrange the pieces and the celery on a warmed platter and keep them warm.

Separate the egg and reserve the white for another use. Beat the cream and egg yolk together. Add a little of the hot sauce from the casserole and mix well, then, stirring constantly, turn the liaison into the rest of the sauce in the casserole. Bring the sauce just to the boiling point but do not let it boil. Season to taste. Spoon the sauce over the birds. Serve with wild rice or hominy.

Rabbit with Lentil Purée

6 to 8 portions

1	rabbit, about 5 pounds fresh, 4½ pounds frozen	1	Bouquet Garni (see Volume 1 Index)
2	cups Brandy Marinade (see Index)	6	tablespoons butter
8	ounces dried lentils		salt
1	small onion		fresh-ground black pepper
1	celery rib	8	slices of firm white bread

If the rabbit is freshly killed, dress, skin, and cut into serving pieces. If it is frozen, let it defrost in the package in the refrigerator. This will take about 36 hours. Rinse the pieces and pat dry. Place them in a ceramic or glass container and pour the marinade over them. Turn to moisten all the pieces. Cover and marinate in a cool place or in the refrigerator for 4 hours for frozen rabbit or 8 hours or overnight for fresh rabbit. Meanwhile, pick over and rinse the dried lentils and soak them in cold water to cover overnight.

Lift rabbit from the marinade and put the pieces in a large stewpot. Peel and chop the onion; wash, trim and chop the celery. Add onion, celery and *bouquet garni* to the stewpot. Strain any remaining marinade into the pot and add enough water to cover the rabbit by 1 inch. Cover the pot and bring the water to a boil. Reduce to a simmer and cook the rabbit for 1½ hours. Drain lentils, rinse them and add to the rabbit. Continue to cook for about 1 hour longer or until both the rabbit and the lentils are tender.

Lift the rabbit pieces out of the liquid and keep warm on a heated platter. Drain the vegetables and lentils, reserving the cooking liquid, and rub through a sieve to make a purée, or purée them through a food mill, or process them in batches in a blender or food processor. Put the purée in a clean saucepan. Add enough of the cooking liquid to give the purée the consistency of a thick sauce. Stir in 2 tablespoons of the butter and season to taste.

Return rabbit to the pot and reheat it gently. Meanwhile, melt remaining butter in a skillet over low heat. Cut the crusts off the bread and cut each slice into 4 triangles. Raise heat slightly and sauté the bread until golden on both sides. Arrange the rabbit on a large platter, spoon the lentil purée over and around it, and arrange the bread triangles around the edge of the platter.

Rabbit with Prunes

6 to 8 portions

1	rabbit, about 5 pounds fresh, 4½ pounds frozen		1	cup dry white wine
2	cups Brandy Marinade (see Index)		1	cup Game Stock (see Index) or Chicken Stock (see Volume 1 Index) or canned broth
8	ounces pitted dried prunes			salt
2	cups strained cold tea			fresh-ground black pepper
3	tablespoons bacon fat			
2	tablespoons flour			

If the rabbit is freshly killed, dress, skin, and cut it into serving pieces. If it is frozen, let it defrost in the package in the refrigerator. This will take about 36 hours. Most frozen rabbit is sold already cut up; if you wish, cut these pieces into smaller portions. Rinse the pieces and pat dry. Place them in a ceramic or glass container and pour the brandy marinade over them. Turn to moisten all the pieces. Cover and marinate in a cool place or in the refrigerator for 4 hours for frozen rabbit, or 8 hours or overnight for fresh rabbit. At the same time soak the prunes in the cold tea.

Remove rabbit pieces from the marinade and pat dry. Strain the marinade and reserve it. Preheat oven to 350°F. Melt the bacon fat in a flameproof 3-quart casserole over low heat. Add the rabbit pieces, a few at a time, and brown on all sides. Remove each batch to a plate as it is done. Sprinkle the flour into the casserole and brown it, stirring, over low heat. Pour in the wine and stock and stir well. Return the rabbit pieces to the casserole and add the soaked prunes. Pour in the strained marinade. Cover the casserole and place it on a rack in the middle level of the oven. Pot-roast wild rabbit for about 2 hours, frozen domestic rabbit for about 1½ hours.

When the rabbit is tender, lift out the pieces and the prunes. Reduce the cooking liquid by boiling it rapidly until you have about 1½ cups. Check the seasoning and add additional seasoning if needed. Return rabbit pieces and prunes to the casserole and reheat them before serving the dish directly from the casserole.

Braised Duck with Ginger and Almonds

4 portions

2	ounces dried black mushrooms
1	duck, 5 to 6 pounds
3	tablespoons peanut oil
2	ounces fresh gingerroot
8	fat scallions

8	sprigs of parsley or coriander (Chinese parsley)
3	tablespoons dark soy sauce
1	cup Chicken Stock (see Volume 1 Index) or canned broth
6	ounces blanched almonds

Soak the mushrooms in 1 cup water for 30 minutes. Rinse mushrooms, discard the stems, and cut the caps into small pieces. Pour the soaking liquid through a coffee filter or fine sieve into a clean bowl and set aside. Cut the duck into 8 pieces. With a cleaver, chop the breasts and thighs into smaller pieces. Remove any bone splinters.

Pour 1 tablespoon of the oil into a deep heavy skillet and brown the duck pieces, a few at a time, until most of the fat is released from the skin. Transfer each batch of duck to a thick layer of paper towels so that more fat is absorbed. Peel the gingerroot. Wash and trim scallions. Wash and dry the parsley. Cut gingerroot, scallions and parsley into small chunks and chop them together in a food processor fitted with the steel blade, or chop with a chef's knife into very small pieces.

Heat the rest of the oil in a flameproof casserole and sauté the chopped gingerroot mixture until the scallions are beginning to turn golden. Place the duck pieces in the casserole and pour in the filtered or strained mushroom soaking liquid, the soy sauce and ½ cup of the stock. Bring the liquid to a boil, then cover the duck pieces closely with a sheet of foil and cover the casserole. Braise the duck on top of the stove or in a 350°F oven, adding more stock if casserole begins to dry. After 1 hour, uncover the casserole and add the soaked mushrooms and the almonds. Gently mix the ingredients. Braise the duck for 30 minutes longer, or until it is tender. Skim any liquid fat on the surface or blot up with paper towels. Serve each portion with a spoonful of the braising liquid and vegetables.

Squabs with Cherries

4 portions

4	squabs, about 1 pound each
1	cup Brandy Marinade (see Index)
2	large shallots
4	tablespoons butter
2	tablespoons olive oil

2	cups Game Stock (see Index), Chicken Stock (see Volume 1 Index) or canned broth
1	Bouquet Garni (see Volume 1 Index)
8	ounces pitted red cherries
4	tablespoons sour cream

Have the squabs dressed and prepared for cooking. Truss them, and place them close together in a ceramic or glass container. Pour the marinade over them and let them marinate at room temperature for 1 hour, turning them at least twice to moisten all sides. Peel and mince the shallots.

Lift the squabs from the marinade and dry them thoroughly. Strain and reserve the marinade. Preheat oven to 350°F. Melt 2 tablespoons of the butter with the oil in a large flameproof casserole set over medium heat. Brown the squabs in the fat on all sides until evenly browned. Transfer the birds to a plate. Sauté the shallots in the casserole until golden. Return squabs to the casserole. Pour in the stock and the strained marinade and add the *bouquet garni*. Cover the casserole and place it on a rack in the middle level of the oven. Braise the squabs for about 1 hour, or until they are done to your taste. Remove the birds from the casserole and use poultry shears to cut them into halves along the backbone. Remove the backbones and discard them and the trussing strings.

Strain the cooking liquids into a clean pan and set it over low heat. Bring to a boil and reduce the sauce by about half. While the sauce is reducing, melt remaining 2 tablespoons butter in a heavy saucepan over low heat. Add the cherries and sauté for 3 minutes. Stir the sour cream into the reduced sauce. Return the squabs to the sauce to reheat them. Turn squabs and sauce into a large serving bowl and scatter the cherries over them.

Note: If the sauce is not thick enough after reducing it, add *beurre manié* (see page 34), 1 teaspoon at a time, before stirring in the sour cream. If you are using canned cherries, be sure to drain them well before sautéing them.

Spanish-Style Chicken

6 portions

1	roasting chicken, 4½ to 5 pounds		4	tablespoons olive oil
1	large onion		1¼	cups Chicken Stock (see Volume 1 Index) or canned broth
2	garlic cloves		8	ounces mushrooms
1	red bell pepper		6	tomatoes, about 2 pounds
1	green bell pepper		10	stuffed green olives
½	cup flour		10	pitted black olives
1	teaspoon salt		2	tablespoons butter
½	teaspoon fresh-ground black pepper			

Cut the chicken into 6 pieces. The giblets can be used to make stock for this recipe or can be stored for another use. Peel and mince the onion. Peel garlic and put through a press into the onion. Halve both peppers, discard stems, seeds and ribs, and chop the peppers. Preheat oven to 325°F.

Season flour with salt and pepper and pour into a sturdy plastic bag; shake well. Shake the chicken pieces, two at a time, in the bag of flour until well coated. Shake off any excess. Heat the oil in a large skillet over moderate heat. Add chicken pieces and brown them for 5 to 7 minutes on each side. Using tongs, transfer chicken pieces to a 2-quart casserole. Add the onion, garlic and peppers to the skillet and cook them, stirring, for 5 to 6 minutes. Spoon the vegetables over the chicken pieces in the casserole.

Pour the stock into a small saucepan and bring it to a boil over moderate heat. Pour the boiling stock into the casserole and cover the casserole. Bake the chicken for 1½ hours, until the leg portions are tender when pierced with a fork. While the chicken is cooking wipe mushrooms with damp paper towels, trim base of stems, and slice caps and stems. Wash and core tomatoes and cut into thick slices; place the slices on a plate and let them drain. Halve both green and black olives. Ten minutes before the chicken is ready, melt the butter in a skillet over medium heat and cook the sliced mushrooms and tomatoes for about 5 minutes. Add mushrooms, tomatoes and olives to the casserole. Serve the chicken and vegetables hot, from the casserole.

Country Chicken Casserole

4 portions

4	chicken quarters, from fryers
3	tablespoons bacon fat, or 2 tablespoons butter and 1 tablespoon oil
	salt
	fresh-ground black pepper
1	small onion
1	celery rib
2	lean bacon strips
3	ripe tomatoes
1	tablespoon flour
1	cup Chicken Stock (see Volume 1 Index) or canned broth
1	cup cooked green peas

Rinse the chicken pieces and dry thoroughly. Preheat oven to 350°F. Heat the fat in a flameproof casserole over medium heat. Starting skin side down, brown the chicken pieces until golden on both sides, about 10 minutes. Sprinkle the browned pieces with salt and pepper. Meanwhile, peel and chop the onion. Wash, trim, and slice the celery. Cut the bacon into narrow strips. Blanch the tomatoes for 10 seconds in boiling water to cover. Peel the tomatoes and cut them into quarters.

Transfer the seasoned chicken pieces to a plate. Put onion, bacon and celery into the casserole and sauté gently for 5 minutes, stirring occasionally. Off the heat, sprinkle the flour into the casserole, then cook and stir until the roux is pale brown. Heat the stock. Off the heat, pour the hot stock into the roux, stirring all the while. Bring to a boil, still stirring. Cook until the sauce is smooth and slightly thickened. Return chicken pieces to the casserole and add the quartered tomatoes. Cover casserole tightly and place on a rack in the middle level of the oven. Braise the chicken for 40 minutes, or until it is as tender as you like it.

About 5 minutes before serving, add the cooked peas to the casserole to heat them. If there is a layer of fat floating on top of the casserole, skim it off or absorb with paper towels. Check the seasoning of the sauce. Serve the chicken and vegetables from the casserole.

Chicken Fricassee

4 portions

4	chicken pieces, each 6 to 8 ounces
3	tablespoons butter
2	tablespoons olive oil
2	large onions
1	tablespoon flour
2	cups Chicken Stock (see Volume 1 Index) or canned broth
1	egg yolk (optional)
3	tablespoons heavy cream (optional)

Rinse the chicken pieces in cold water and dry them thoroughly. Heat the butter and oil in a large skillet over moderate heat. Starting skin side down, sear the chicken pieces for about 15 minutes, until they are golden all over. Do not let them brown. Transfer chicken to a flameproof casserole. Peel the onions and chop fine. Sauté them in the fat remaining in the skillet for about 10 minutes, stirring occasionally, until they are soft, translucent and golden, but not browned. Off the heat stir the flour into the onions in the skillet. Return pan to heat and cook, stirring, until the roux is just golden. Pour the stock into the skillet and stir well to deglaze the pan. Bring the mixture to a boil, then pour it over the chicken

pieces in the casserole. Cover the casserole, set over medium-low heat, and simmer for about 1 hour, until the chicken is tender. Skim off any surface fat.

The chicken can be served as is, or the sauce can be enriched and thickened with an egg and cream liaison. To do this, first transfer the chicken to a platter. Then beat the egg yolk and cream together, warm the mixture with a little of the hot sauce from the casserole, and turn the liaison into the casserole. Let the mixture come to the boiling point, then remove from heat or set over very low heat and stir until the sauce is well blended. Pour sauce over the chicken and serve at once, with hot biscuits.

Braised Chicken with Herbs

4 to 6 portions

1	roasting chicken, 4 pounds		2	tablespoons chopped parsley
2	garlic cloves		2	tablespoons chopped scallions
4	ounces mushrooms			
4	tablespoons butter		1	tablespoon dried tarragon
1	lemon		1	teaspoon dried marjoram
1¼	cups Chicken Stock (see Volume 1 Index) or canned broth		½	teaspoon salt
			¼	teaspoon fresh-ground black pepper

Cut the chicken into serving pieces. Peel garlic and put through a press into a bowl. Wipe mushrooms with a damp cloth or paper towels, trim base of stems, and slice caps and stems. Preheat oven to 325°F.

Melt the butter in a large skillet over medium heat. Brown the chicken pieces in the butter on all sides, turning them with tongs or 2 large spoons. While the chicken is browning, juice the lemon. Remove chicken from the skillet and place the pieces on the bottom of a 2-quart casserole. Pour the stock into the skillet and stir well to deglaze it. Bring

the liquid to a boil over high heat. Add the parsley, chopped scallions, tarragon and marjoram to the pressed garlic. Mix the herbs, then stir them into the stock. Add the mushrooms, lemon juice, salt and pepper to the chicken in the casserole and pour the stock and herb mixture over the chicken. The chicken should not be covered with liquid. Cover the casserole tightly and place it on a rack in the middle level of the oven. Braise the chicken for 1½ hours, or until the leg portions are tender. Serve from the casserole, over buttered noodles or rice.

Turkey Pot-Roasted in Beer

4 to 6 portions

4	turkey legs, each about 1 pound	1	cup Tomato Sauce (see Volume 4 Index)
4	tablespoons peanut oil		salt
1	large onion		fresh-ground black pepper
2	garlic cloves	12	ounces beer
1	large green pepper	½	teaspoon Tabasco

Rinse turkey legs and pat dry. Heat 2 tablespoons of the oil in a skillet large enough to hold 2 turkey legs at a time. Brown the turkey legs on all sides over medium heat. Brown remaining turkey legs in the same way. Transfer them to a platter. Pour off the fat in the skillet. Preheat oven to 350°F.

Peel the onion and garlic. Wash the pepper, peel it with a swivel vegetable peeler, and discard stem, seeds and ribs. Chop onion, garlic and green pepper by hand to even-size pieces the size of a green pea. Heat remaining oil in the skillet over medium heat and sauté the chopped vegetables until the onion is translucent and golden. Pour in the tomato sauce and mix well. Turn the mixture into a heavy casserole. Sprinkle the turkey legs with salt and pepper and add them to the vegetables. Pour in the beer and the Tabasco. Bring the liquid to a boil, cover the casserole, and place it on a rack in the middle level of the oven. Pot-roast the turkey for 1¼ to 1½ hours, or until it is almost falling off the bones.

Lift the turkey legs to a carving board and cut the meat off the bones. Discard bones and the long pieces of cartilage. Return turkey to the sauce and reheat it. Serve dish directly from the casserole, spooning turkey and sauce over rice.

Andalusian Chicken

(Chicken from the South of Spain)

6 portions

1	roasting chicken, about 4½ pounds	1	cup Chicken Stock (see Volume 1 Index) or canned broth
2	cups cooked rice	2	large bell peppers, red and green or both green
½	cup diced cooked ham	1	pound tomatoes
2	teaspoons paprika		fresh-ground black pepper
	salt	1	scant tablespoon flour
2	large onions	2	tablespoons tomato purée
4	tablespoons butter	½	cup white wine
3	tablespoons olive oil		
1	Bouquet Garni (see Volume 1 Index)		

Rinse the chicken inside and out and dry thoroughly. Mix the cooked rice, ham, paprika and 1 teaspoon salt together; stuff the chicken with the mixture. Fold the neck skin over and fasten with a skewer. Truss the bird (see page 28 of Volume 2).

Peel one of the onions and cut it into halves. Heat 2 tablespoons of the butter and 1 tablespoon of the oil in a skillet. Brown the chicken on all sides, until evenly golden. Transfer the bird to a flameproof casserole just large enough to hold it. Put the onion halves around it and add the *bouquet garni*. Pour in ½ cup of the stock. Bring the stock to a boil, reduce heat, cover the casserole, and braise the chicken for about 1 hour, until it is tender. Add more of the stock during the cooking if it all evaporates. The chicken should not stick to the bottom or become too brown on the bottom.

While the chicken is braising, prepare the garnish. Peel remaining onion, cut it into thick slices, and separate the slices into rings. Wash the peppers, cut out the stems, and scoop out the seeds and ribs. Cut the peppers across into rings. Blanch the tomatoes; peel, halve, and seed them. Discard seeds and chop tomatoes. Heat remaining butter and oil in the skillet used for browning the chicken. Sauté the onion rings in it for 3 minutes or until they are translucent but not browned. Add the peppers, tomatoes, 1 teaspoon salt and 5 grindings of pepper, and cook gently until the vegetables are soft; however, both onion rings and pepper rings should keep their shape. Set aside and keep warm.

Remove chicken from the pot and place on a heated serving platter. Remove the skewer and trussing strings. Surround the bird with the garnish. Discard the onion halves and the *bouquet garni* from the casserole. Place the casserole over high heat and sprinkle in the flour, stirring constantly with a wooden spoon. Stir in the tomato purée and the wine. Still stirring, bring sauce to a boil and stir to deglaze the casserole. Strain the sauce over the chicken and serve immediately.

Pot-Roasted Chicken with Wine and Cheese

6 portions

6	chicken breast halves, each about 6 ounces		½	teaspoon salt
4	tablespoons vegetable oil		3½	teaspoons dried mixed herbs
2	teaspoons whole cloves		8	ounces Gruyère cheese
2	cups Marsala			

Preheat oven to 350°F. Skin the chicken breasts. Heat the oil in a large heavy skillet over moderate heat. Add the chicken breasts and sauté them, turning them frequently, for 4 to 5 minutes, until they are evenly browned on all sides. Use tongs to remove chicken from the pan and drain the pieces on paper towels. Insert 5 or 6 cloves into each chicken breast, spacing them evenly over the surface of the meat. Place the chicken in a large ovenproof casserole. Pour in 1½ cups of the wine and add the salt and herbs. Cover the casserole. Pot-roast the chicken for 1 hour, or until it is tender. Baste the tops frequently with remaining wine. Grate the cheese. Remove casserole from the oven and uncover it. Sprinkle a thick layer of the cheese over the chicken. Return the casserole, uncovered, to the oven and bake for 15 minutes longer, until the cheese is melted and golden brown. Serve at once. *Note:* Marsala wine is available dry and sweet. The flavor of the dish will be determined by the kind you choose. Use fewer cloves if you like a less pungent flavor. The herb mixture can be any that you like. Try a mixture of parsley, thyme and marjoram, with a little grated lemon rind.

Chicken Mandarin

4 portions

1	large frying chicken, 3½ pounds	½	cup peanut oil
½	cup flour	½	cup Chicken Stock (see Volume 1 Index) or canned broth
½	teaspoon salt		
½	teaspoon fresh-ground black pepper	3	tablespoons medium-dry sherry
½	teaspoon paprika	2	tablespoons soy sauce
3	scallions	2	teaspoons white-wine vinegar
1	large green pepper		
1	garlic clove	1	teaspoon dry mustard
1	can (11 ounces) mandarin orange sections	2	teaspoons cornstarch

Cut the chicken into 4 serving pieces. Spoon the flour into a sturdy plastic bag and add the salt, pepper and paprika; shake to mix well. Wash and trim the scallions and chop them. Wash and halve the green pepper. Remove stem, seeds and ribs, and chop the pepper. Peel the garlic clove and put it on a wooden toothpick. Pour off and reserve ½ cup of the juice from the canned mandarins, and drain off the rest. If there is less than ½ cup of juice, add orange juice or water to make up the difference.

Shake the chicken quarters, one at a time, in the bag of seasoned flour until well coated; shake off any excess. Heat the oil in a large flameproof casserole over medium heat. When oil is hot, add the chicken pieces and cook, turning occasionally with tongs, for 8 to 12 minutes to brown them evenly. Use tongs to remove the pieces from the casserole; set them aside. Add the scallions, green pepper and garlic to the casserole and sauté them, stirring occasionally, for 8 minutes. Discard the garlic. Preheat oven to 350°F.

In a mixing bowl combine the reserved orange juice, the stock, sherry, soy sauce, vinegar and mustard; stir to mix. Add the liquid to the casserole and stir to blend with the vegetables. Return chicken pieces and turn them to coat with the liquid. Cover the casserole. Braise the chicken, stirring and coating the pieces occasionally, for about 45 minutes, until the legs are tender when pierced with the point of a knife. Using tongs, transfer chicken quarters to a warmed serving plate.

Make a paste of the cornstarch and 1 tablespoon cold water. Set the casserole over medium heat and bring the liquid again to a boil. Stir in the cornstarch paste and cook, still stirring, until the sauce is thick and translucent. Stir in the mandarin orange sections and cook for 3 minutes, stirring occasionally. Pour the sauce over the chicken pieces and serve at once.

Danish Chicken with Cheese

4 to 6 portions

1	roasting chicken, 5 pounds	1¼	cups Chicken Stock (see Volume 1 Index) or canned broth
½	cup flour		
1	teaspoon salt		
½	teaspoon fresh-ground black pepper	1	medium-size green pepper
		2	tomatoes
2	teaspoons dried dill	2	ounces Samsoe or Cheddar cheese
2	eggs		
4	tablespoons butter	½	cup heavy cream
2	tablespoons vegetable oil		

Cut the chicken into 8 serving pieces and remove all the skin. (Wing tips, neck and giblets can be used to make stock for this recipe or stored for another time.) Combine the flour,

salt, pepper and crumbled dried dill in a sturdy plastic bag and shake to mix well. Beat the eggs lightly. Dip the chicken pieces first into the beaten eggs, then shake them, a few pieces at a time, in the bag of flour, until well coated. Shake off any excess.

Melt the butter with the oil in a large flameproof casserole over medium heat. Add the chicken pieces and brown them on all sides for about 8 minutes, turning them frequently with tongs or large spoons. Pour the chicken stock into the casserole and bring it to a boil. Reduce heat to low, cover the casserole, and braise the chicken gently for 40 minutes, until tender when pierced with the point of a sharp knife. Meanwhile, wash the green pepper, remove the stem, and scoop out seeds and ribs. Cut the pepper crosswise into rings. Blanch tomatoes for 30 seconds in boiling water to cover, and peel the tomatoes and cut each one into 4 to 6 slices. Grate the cheese.

With a slotted spoon lift the chicken pieces from the casserole, set aside and keep warm while finishing the dish. Preheat broiler and set tray about 4 inches from heat source. Add green pepper rings to the liquid in the casserole and simmer for 4 minutes. Add tomato slices, stir gently to combine and cook for 2 minutes longer. With a slotted spoon transfer vegetables to the platter and arrange them around the chicken pieces.

Remove casserole from heat and stir the cream into the liquid. Return to heat and cook gently for 2 to 3 minutes, still stirring. Return chicken to the casserole and spoon sauce over it. Sprinkle the grated cheese on top and place the casserole under the broiler for 5 minutes, until cheese is bubbling. Serve immediately.

Part Three

HOMEMADE FILLED PASTA

"... when confronted by a piece of homemade pasta, Italian cooks
can't resist the temptation to invent a filling, a shape and a name."

The Romagnolis' Table

Whether it is true that every housewife in Italy makes her own fresh pasta daily, it is certainly true that there are some types of pasta dishes that absolutely require it. When made with egg-rich, golden-hued home-made dough, filled pasta dishes—lasagne, cannelloni, ravioli—can completely transcend the ordinary stodgy fare that most of us have come to expect when they are served to us.

The very best pasta dough is not only homemade, but handmade as well, in the sense that it is kneaded and rolled out by hand. Dough for pasta is still best done the old-fashioned way. An honest ten-minute kneading and hand-rolling will produce a dough far superior in every way to any dough that comes out of a machine. There is the familiar hand-cranked pasta machine—the one that looks like a miniature clothes wringer—and there is also a more expensive, electrically powered version. Although both will save a great deal of time, the process tends to give the pasta a smooth, slippery surface that doesn't hold the sauce nearly as well as does the hand-rolled kind, whose irregularities of form and texture are so prized by connoisseurs.

The simplest of the filled pastas, though it is not really filled, but rather layered with filling, is lasagne. In America, lasagne most frequently is the type that comes from Bologna, in which the pasta is layered with a meat sauce, a béchamel sauce, and cheese—always Parmesan, and often mozzarella and ricotta. But there is in Italy an endless number of variations on the basic lasagne theme. Lasagne can include eggplant, zucchini, peppers, sausages, olives, capers, anchovies, meatballs, and even hard-cooked eggs. It can be a catchall casserole in which to recycle leftovers or it can be a very simple and elegant assembly of ingredients designed to highlight a single seasonal specialty such as truffles or wild boletus mushrooms. Marcella Hazan states unequivocally that in Italy, no matter what type is prepared, "Lasagne is never, but simply never, made with anything but homemade pasta dough." (*The Classic Italian Cookbook*) Here, sadly, the reverse is usually true.

Pasta for cannelloni is made exactly as for lasagne, but the strips are shorter and each pasta rectangle is rolled around a layer of filling to enclose it like a little crêpe. The individual rolls are tucked in a shallow casserole and blanketed with rich sauces and cheese, to be baked to a golden bubbling perfection.

Perhaps the most appealing of all filled pastas are the individual squares of ravioli and the hand-shaped tortellini and cappelletti. All over Italy one can find delicious little pasta bundles filled with every imaginable kind of filling.

Ravioli, filled with meat or cheese and served with some sort of tomato sauce, are perhaps the most familiar of these pasta packages, although few people are likely to consider them a delicacy until they have tasted the fresh, homemade, hand-made variety.

Tortellini, sometimes called Venus's navels because of their shape, are coiled half-moons of stuffed pasta that are another specialty of Bologna.

Cappelletti are essentially tortellini shaped into coiled, pinched triangles instead of crescents. They are considered to bear a likeness to bishops' hats and are the traditional Christmas Eve dish in Perugia.

Undoubtedly these homemade pasta packages are something of a luxury in our hectic day and age. Not exactly a luxury in terms of expense, but a luxury in that they are time-consuming to make. Indeed, the process can be likened to a craft like quilting, in terms of both the skill and patience required and in the ultimate rewards and accolades that are garnered.

Filled pasta can be served in many ways, but in Italy it is most commonly served in small portions as a first course. Cappelletti and tortellini are often served in a clear broth with an additional garnish of freshly ground pepper and grated Parmesan cheese. But they are also served quite on their own, adorned with only a little butter and a grating of cheese, or in a special sauce.

There is something universally appealing about filled pastas—perhaps it is the element of surprise, or the contrasting textures of filling and pasta wrapping, or even some private pride or pleasure in the slightly greater amount of care and trouble that has been taken. Whatever the reason, they are unfailingly popular, and once you have served them to your guests you will know for a fact that you can never make enough of them.

Because of all the work that they involve, homemade filled pastas are usually special-occasion dishes. But no one ever said you had to do it all alone. Try it the way Francesco Ghedini suggests, ". . . with four good tempered people working together: one to make the dough, a sheet at a time so that the dough doesn't get too dry, and three others to sit around the table stuffing, folding and gossiping." (*Northern Italian Cooking*)

HOMEMADE FILLED PASTA

Nothing equals the delicate taste and tender, melt-in-your mouth texture of homemade pasta filled with a rich and savory stuffing. Making your own egg-rich pasta dough is not at all difficult, and although it may take a little practice to roll out perfect lasagne noodles and shape your own tortellini, the results will be so satisfying and impressive that you will find that the extra time spent on preparing these dishes is well rewarded indeed.

The observation of a few simple guidelines will help the beginning pasta chef produce successful and delicious results on the very first try.

Making the Dough

The dough for filled pasta is a basic mixture of flour, eggs and salt with a little bit of olive oil added for tenderness. Sometimes it may be necessary to add a small amount of water as well.

The general rule calls for 1 large egg for every ¾ cup of flour. However, since the amount of humidity in the atmosphere varies from day to day, so does the amount of liquid that the flour will absorb. Although it is almost impossible for a recipe to specify exactly how much water (if any) you will need to make a workable dough, you will quickly learn to judge from experience.

Spinach Pasta

Spinach is sometimes added to pasta dough. Italians call this *pasta verde,* or green pasta. The spinach does not really add much flavor to the pasta but it does make the dough softer and more tender. When it comes to kneading and rolling out the pasta this is a special bonus to the cook who is a beginner, so many cooking classes start novice pasta makers off with a spinach dough. Spinach pasta dough may be substituted in any of the recipes that call for regular pasta dough, and it makes an extremely attractive presentation when alternated with layers of regular pasta in baked lasagne dishes. You may use fresh or frozen spinach but it should be cooked until tender, refreshed under cold running water, drained, squeezed to remove excess moisture, and chopped very fine by hand or in a food processor.

The spinach should be added to the flour together with the eggs and olive oil. As it provides extra moisture, you will probably not need to add water to the dough. You may, in fact, want to add a little extra flour when you are kneading to bring the pasta to the correct texture.

Kneading the Dough

Knead the dough on a well-floured work surface. Dust both hands with flour and work the dough, pressing down with the heel of your hand, folding the dough, turning it, and pressing down and away again. The dough should be kneaded for at least 10 minutes, until it feels smooth and satiny. Once again, experience will be your best teacher, and after you have done this a few times, you will know exactly what "smooth and satiny" means. The dough should feel slightly damp, with a texture that is resilient and feels alive.

A note on the food processor: Unfortunately, the food processor does not produce the proper consistency of dough for homemade pasta. You may use it to mix the initial ingredients, but you will still have to knead the dough by hand.

After the dough is kneaded and before it is rolled out, it should be allowed to rest, covered with plastic wrap, a towel, or an overturned bowl. The rest period "relaxes" the dough (as well as the cook) and makes it possible for you to roll it out to the degree of thinness desired. Let it rest for at least 30 minutes, or as long as 2 or 3 hours in a cool, dry place.

Rolling Out the Dough

This is one of the most important steps in making your own pasta and requires practice to get the pasta as thin and pliable as it should be. The pasta dough must be rolled and stretched until it is paper-thin and feels like a sheet of fine fabric. This is the quality that will set it apart from coarser machine-manufactured pasta. Fortunately, even your very first attempts will be far superior to the packaged variety.

It will be easier to roll out the dough if you divide it into halves, thirds or even quarters, depending on the quantity of dough, and work with one section at a time. Roll each section into a ball and cover the pieces so they do not dry out.

You will need a large uncluttered work area with a smooth surface on which to roll your dough. You will also need a sturdy rolling pin. Many experienced pasta makers prefer the long slim European type of rolling pin that has no ball bearings or other mechanical parts and resembles a truncated broom handle.

Place the ball of dough you are rolling on the lightly floured work surface. Dust your hands with flour and press down on the dough with your palms to shape the dough into a rectangle that is approximately 1 inch thick. Dust the rolling pin with flour and use it to press the dough away from you with a rolling-stretching motion. Do this two or three times, then lift the dough and give it a quarter turn. Continue to roll and stretch in the same manner, turning the dough from time to time and always making sure that there is enough flour under the dough to keep it from sticking. The final sheet of pasta should be almost transparent and extremely supple. Cover the rolled-out dough with a towel while you roll out the rest.

You can gather up any leftover scraps of dough, roll them into a ball,

Making Fresh Pasta Dough

approximately 1 pound

3	cups all-purpose flour
1	teaspoon salt
4	large eggs
2	tablespoons olive oil
2	to 4 tablespoons warm water
	additional flour as needed
¾	pound fresh spinach or 1 10-ounce package frozen leaf spinach (optional)

For spinach pasta: Pick over fresh spinach and discard tough stems and damaged leaves. Wash thoroughly and place in large saucepan. Set over medium heat and cover and cook in the water clinging to the leaves, for about 10 minutes, or until just tender. If using frozen spinach, allow to thaw at room temperature, then cook with salt in a covered saucepan for 3 to 5 minutes. Refresh the spinach under cold running water. Drain and then squeeze the excess moisture from the spinach. Purée spinach in food processor or food mill. Add to the flour together with eggs and olive oil (see Step 3). The pasta dough will be green in color and very tender. You may need to add a few tablespoons more flour if dough is very moist.

Note: You can prepare half the amount of pasta dough (½ pound) by cutting all the ingredients in the recipe in half. To increase the recipe, remember to allow ¾ cup of flour for each large egg. Increase everything else proportionately.

1 Sift flour and salt into a bowl. Make a well and pour eggs and olive oil into the well.

2 Beat eggs with fork, gradually mixing in flour to make a stiff crumbly dough. Add a little extra water, if necessary (omit for spinach pasta).

3 For spinach pasta, add puréed spinach with eggs and olive oil and mix well.

4 Remove dough to a floured work surface and press dough into a ball.

5 Knead dough for 10 minutes, until it is smooth, firm and satiny to the touch.

6 Wrap dough in wax paper or in plastic wrap or cover with a bowl and let rest in a cool dry place for a minimum of 30 minutes, or up to 3 hours.

let them rest, covered, for 10 to 15 minutes, and roll out again.

A note on pasta machines: There are many pasta machines available on the market, some operated manually, others, more expensive, electrically. After the dough is kneaded, the pasta machine is used to roll out the dough to the desired thickness. A pasta machine is certainly a labor-saving device and will produce pasta vastly superior to the store-bought variety, but almost all experts agree that pasta rolled out by machine does not equal the quality and tenderness of pasta rolled out by hand.

Preparing Lasagne

Careful organization and orderly procedure will simplify the process of preparing and assembling a homemade lasagne. The filling and sauce should be at room temperature or cooler.

Choose a rectangular baking dish that is at least 2½ inches deep. Some specialty cookware shops carry imported lasagne pans with squared-off corners and a depth of 3 inches. These are ideal, but almost any roasting pan is suitable. Before rolling your dough, measure the length of the pan to determine the length of your lasagne sheets. Grease the pan and set aside.

Roll out the pasta dough as thin as possible and cut into strips that are approximately 3 inches wide and long enough to fit snugly into the baking pan.

Bring 4 quarts of water to a boil and add 2 tablespoons of salt and 1 tablespoon of olive oil. While the water is heating, soak a large towel in cold water, wring it out, and lay it flat on your work counter. Have a bowl of cold water near your stove.

Drop strips of pasta into boiling water, no more than 4 at a time, and cook for 15 to 20 seconds, stirring all the while with a long wooden spoon. Remove the strips with a large slotted spoon and plunge them immediately into the waiting bowl of cold water. Swirl them around to cool, remove them, and lay them out flat on the

Rolling Out Pasta Dough

1 Press down and flatten the dough into a rectangular or oval shape.

2 Roll dough away from you, pressing and stretching to make a thin rectangular or oval sheet.

3 Use a sharp knife to cut the dough into strips of the desired width.

3 Unravel the noodles and lay out flat on a board or clean work surface.

damp towel while you prepare the others.

To assemble the lasagne, spread a thin layer of sauce on the bottom of the pan and then cover it with strips of cooked pasta, letting the strips overlap slightly so that no spaces are left in between.

More sauce and cheese come next, followed by another layer of pasta. Continue building the lasagne in this manner but do not exceed 6 layers of pasta. The lasagne should be finished off with a thin layer of sauce and a topping of cheese and then baked according to the instructions in the recipe.

A note on freezing lasagne: The assembled lasagne can be wrapped in foil and frozen successfully for future use. Allow frozen lasagne to come to room temperature before baking.

Making Cannelloni

The pasta for cannelloni is prepared in exactly the same way as for lasagne, but the strips are shorter so that they can be rolled around a filling instead of layered. Cannelloni are the simplest to make of the stuffed pastas, and can be among the most elegant and delicious dishes in the world. Once again, good organization and the careful following of an orderly sequence of steps will insure success.

 Working quickly, turn dough and roll and stretch until it is paper-thin.

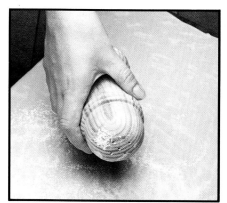 **4** For noodles, lightly flour the top of the rolled-out dough. Roll up like a jelly roll, but do not press on the pasta.

OR For lasagne, cut dough into strips 3 inches wide.

OR For cannelloni, cut the strips into 4-inch lengths and roll around chosen filling.

First prepare the pasta dough, filling and sauce. It is important to have the filling and the sauce at room temperature or cooler.

Then roll out the dough so it is very thin, as for lasagne. Cut into rectangles approximately 3 inches wide by 4 inches long.

Butter an ovenproof baking dish large enough to hold the cannelloni in one layer. Use two baking dishes if you need to so the cannelloni are not stacked one on top of the other.

Bring 4 quarts of water to a boil and add 2 tablespoons salt and 1 tablespoon olive oil. While the water is heating, soak a large towel in cold water, wring it out, and lay it flat on your work counter. Have a bowl of cold water near your stove. Cook cannelloni pasta exactly like the lasagne strips (15 to 20 seconds), then plunge into cold water and drain on the damp towel.

To stuff cannelloni, lay a strip of pasta flat on a large plate and spread 2 tablespoons of filling evenly over the surface, taking care to leave a ½-inch border all around. Roll the cannelloni like crêpes and place side by side in a baking dish, placing the seam side down.

Spread sauce over the cannelloni, sprinkle with cheese, and bake according to recipe instructions.

A note on freezing cannelloni: The assembled cannelloni may be tightly wrapped and frozen for future use. Bring to room temperature before baking.

Making Ravioli, Tortellini and Cappelletti

These small stuffed pasta dumplings are among the most appealing and impressive homemade pasta dishes. But they require a bit of manual dexterity and a lot of patience, for they can't be made in a hurry. On the other hand, there is nothing so difficult about them that you can't enlist the aid of all available children, friends and relatives for a cozy afternoon of stuffing these endearing pasta bundles. Your skills will certainly improve with practice, but even if your first ravioli, tortellini or cappelletti frustrate you because they look a little clumsy and inept, their delicious taste and delicate texture will convince you to make them again and again, and soon they will be as beautiful to the eye as they are to the mouth.

A note on fillings for ravioli, tortellini and cappelletti: While there are a number of traditional fillings—cheese or a combination of cheeses, cheese and herbs or vegetables, meat—this is the kind of preparation that most agreeably lends itself to the play of a cook's imagination and experimentation. In reality, there are as many different kinds of fillings as there are people making and filling their own pasta dumplings. The recipes that follow are a starting point and they will give you a good idea of the general principles and guidelines. But after that you should let your culinary imagination be your guide.

The meat fillings for ravioli, tortellini or cappelletti must be precooked because the filled pasta dumplings are not poached long enough to thoroughly cook raw meat. Before using them, the fillings must be cooled, and most are best after a few hours of refrigeration, so that they are firm enough to work with. A warm wet filling will ooze out of its little envelope, and even an uncooked cheese filling will be firmer and more manageable after a bit of chilling.

Lasagne Bolognese

6 to 8 portions

3½ to 4 cups Bolognese Sauce
(see Volume 4 Index)

8 ounces mozzarella cheese
2 cups Béchamel Sauce (see
Volume 3 Index)

2 tablespoons salt
1 tablespoon olive oil
1 pound pasta dough cut into
lasagne strips

¾ cup (3 ounces) grated
Parmesan cheese

This refined lasagne from Bologna, so different from the more robust lasagnes of southern Italy, is perhaps the most popular lasagne of all, as the meat sauce combines deliciously with the cheese and the cream sauce.

1 Select a dish for the lasagne, coat liberally with butter, and set aside.

2 Bring 4 quarts of water to a boil. Place a bowl of cold water nearby and lay out a damp cloth.

6 Cover pasta with Bolognese sauce. Shred mozzarella cheese in food processor, or cut into thin slices.

7 Dot Bolognese sauce with shredded mozzarella cheese and cover with another layer of pasta.

8 Spread a thin layer of béchamel sauce over the pasta and sprinkle with some of the Parmesan.

Making Ravioli. Divide the kneaded pasta dough into 4 pieces and roll each piece into a ball. Large sheets of pasta are very hard to work with and you may, in fact, prefer to divide each of the four pieces in half again. Remember to keep the waiting dough covered.

Roll out a piece of dough into the thinnest possible oval or rectangle. Roll out a second piece of dough to a simi-lar size and shape and cover it with a damp towel to prevent drying.

Arrange scant teaspoonfuls of filling across and down the first sheet of pasta, leaving a 2-inch space between each spoonful.

Dip a pastry brush in water and lightly paint a square border around each little ball of filling. This will enable the top layer of pasta to stick and form a pocket for the filling.

Gently lift the other sheet of pasta by draping it over your rolling pin and lay it carefully over the first sheet. Align the edges of the two sheets as much as possible and, using your fingers, press down firmly but gently along the damp lines around each bit of filling. Use a pastry wheel or small sharp knife to cut the ravioli squares apart.

Make sure that the edges of all the ravioli squares are firmly sealed. You

Sauces may be made in advance. If you are going to hold the white sauce, cover it with a thin layer of melted but-ter or a round of buttered wax paper to prevent a skin from forming.

Lasagne Bolognese is almost a one-dish meal, since it contains both meat and filling pasta. Serve it alone or with a salad or green vegetable.

3 Add salt and oil to boiling water. Add lasagne strips and boil 15 to 20 seconds. Remove and plunge into bowl of cold water.

4 Drain the lasagne. Spread out on the damp cloth in a single layer to cool.

5 Spread a thin layer of Bolognese sauce on bottom of pan, then cover with a layer of lasagne strips.

9 Repeat the pasta, Bolognese sauce and mozzarella cheese layers. Cover cheese with pasta.

10 Top with remaining Bolognese sauce, béchamel and mozzarella cheese. Sprinkle with remaining Parmesan cheese.

11 Bake on center rack of oven for 15 minutes, or until lasagne is golden and bubbling.

may wish to crimp the edges with the tines of a fork. This is not only an attrac-tive flourish but insures a tighter seal.

Remove the completed ravioli squares to a large floured cookie sheet and keep them covered with a towel dredged in flour. Let them dry for at least an hour before cooking. They may wait longer in a cool, dry place.

Making Tortellini and Cappelletti. These are the most classic exam-ples of the homemade filled pasta dumplings. After the dough is rolled into a thin and pliable sheet, squares or circles are cut out. These are then filled with a dollop of stuffing and folded into a triangle or semicircle. After the edges are firmly sealed, the pointed ends are brought together to form a ring, there-by creating the two classic shapes—little peaked hats (cappelletti) or rounded belly buttons (tortellini).

Work with a small amount of dough at a time. Roll it out as thin as possible.

Cut the dough into 2-inch squares with a knife, or cut out circles with a 2-inch cookie cutter. Place ½ teaspoon of filling in the center of each pasta square or circle. Use a pastry brush to paint the edges with water.

Fold the square or circle across the filling diagonally and press all the

Homemade Cannelloni

4 to 5 portions

The filling	The sauce	

The filling

8   ounces mozzarella cheese
8   ounces ricotta cheese
3   ounces cooked lean ham
2   large eggs
    salt
    fresh-ground black pepper

The sauce

10 tablespoons unsalted butter
2   cups canned peeled plum
    tomatoes
1   teaspoon minced fresh
    basil, or ½ teaspoon
    dried basil
    salt
    fresh-ground black pepper

16 rectangles of fresh pasta,
    each approximately 4 ×
    3 inches
2   tablespoons salt
1   tablespoon olive oil

¼   cup (1 ounce) grated
    Parmesan cheese

3 Stir eggs into ham and cheeses. Season with salt and pepper to taste. Set aside.

4 To prepare sauce, melt 6 tablespoons of the butter in a large skillet. Cut tomatoes into rough cubes.

5 To skillet, add tomatoes, basil, and salt and pepper to taste. Simmer over low heat for 10 minutes, stirring often.

8 Drain pasta, cool in bowl of cold water, and drain. Lay pasta rectangles in single layer on damp towel.

9 Spread 3 tablespoons of filling on each strip of pasta and roll like a crêpe.

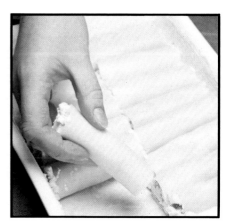

10 Place rolled cannelloni side by side in the buttered baking dish.

edges together with your fingertips. Bring the opposite ends together and press to make a ring.

Place the finished tortellini or cappelletti on a floured cookie sheet and cover with a flour-dredged towel. Let dry for at least 1 hour.

Leftover Filling or Pasta Dough

It is a fact of life that there will always be either filling or pasta dough left over. Don't worry about it; just use the leftovers as follows: Gather pasta bits into a ball, let rest for 10 or 15 minutes, and then roll out and cut into thin noodles for soup. Excess filling can be used in omelets or rolled into balls and poached in soup as dumplings.

Freezing Ravioli, Tortellini and Cappelletti

All filled pasta dumplings may be successfully frozen. Freeze them after they are filled but before they are cooked. Arrange the dumplings so they do not touch on a large wire cake rack that has been brushed with oil. Place rack uncovered in the freezer. The dumplings will freeze quickly and uniformly. When they are completely frozen, remove them and put them in a plastic freezer bag. Frozen dumplings need not be defrosted before cooking; simply add 2 to 3 minutes to the cooking time.

Cooking Ravioli, Tortellini and Cappelletti

Homemade ravioli, tortellini and cappelletti cook very quickly and should be served as soon as possible after they have been cooked.

Bring 4 quarts of water to a boil and add 2 tablespoons salt and 1 tablespoon olive oil. Drop in the dumplings and cook for 5 minutes after the water returns to a boil. Drain, place them immediately in a warmed bowl and toss with butter, cream or sauce.

1 Cut mozzarella cheese into dice and place in a bowl with ricotta cheese.

2 Cut ham into small pieces and add to cheeses. Beat eggs until frothy.

6 Preheat oven to 400°F. Coat a shallow ovenproof dish with 2 tablespoons of the butter.

7 Drop pasta, a few pieces at a time, into 4 quarts boiling water to which salt and oil have been added. Cook 15 to 20 seconds. Soak towel in cold water and wring out.

11 Pour sauce over cannelloni and sprinkle with cheese. Dot with remaining 2 tablespoons butter.

12 Bake on center rack of oven for 15 to 20 minutes, until sauce is bubbly and cheese is golden.

Homemade Ravioli

6 to 8 portions

The filling

3 tablespoons unsalted butter
1 medium-size onion
1 pound lean ground veal
1 10-ounce package fresh
  spinach
½ cup (2 ounces) grated
  Parmesan cheese
¼ teaspoon freshly grated
  nutmeg
1 garlic clove
1 egg
¼ teaspoon dried orégano
  salt
  fresh-ground black pepper

1 pound fresh pasta dough
2 tablespoons salt
1 tablespoon olive oil

6 tablespoons unsalted butter
½ cup (2 ounces) grated
  Parmesan cheese
  or
2 cups Tomato Sauce (see
  Volume 4 Index)

1 Melt butter in a heavy skillet over low heat. Peel and mince onion. Add onion and cook, stirring, for 4 minutes.

2 Add ground veal and cook over medium heat, stirring frequently, until meat loses its pink color and moisture has evaporated.

6 Cover one rectangle with a damp towel while you place scant teaspoons of filling at 2-inch intervals down and across the other rectangle of pasta dough.

7 Use a pastry brush to brush all the spaces between and around the mounds of filling with cold water.

Making Tortellini

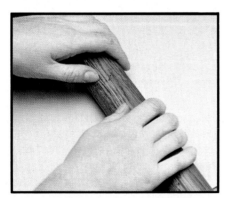

1 Roll out fresh pasta to a paper-thin sheet.

2 Use a 2-inch cookie cutter to stamp out circles.

3 Wet edges of each circle with cold water, using a pastry brush.

3 Wash and cook spinach, drain, refresh and squeeze dry. Purée in food processor. Mix onion, veal, spinach, cheese and nutmeg. Chop garlic fine and add.

4 Beat in egg, orégano, salt and pepper to taste. Refrigerate until needed.

5 Divide dough into 4 equal portions. Cover 3. Halve remaining piece. Roll into 2 rectangles approximately 16 inches by 10 inches and ⅛ inch thick.

8 Place the second piece of rolled-out dough on top and press it to the lower sheet around the edges and between the mounds of filling.

9 Use a pastry wheel to cut the ravioli squares apart. Put on floured cookie sheet, cover with flour-dredged towel, and let dry for 1 hour.

10 Add salt and oil to boiling water. Cook ravioli for 5 minutes. Drain and serve with butter and cheese or homemade tomato sauce.

4 Place ½ teaspoon of filling in the center of each round of dough.

5 Fold edges of the round together and gently press the moistened rim so the edges stick together.

6 Wrap the straight edge of each half-moon around your finger and press together. Seal with a drop of water.

Vegetarian Lasagne with Spinach-Cheese Filling

4 to 6 portions

The sauce

2	medium-size onions
2	garlic cloves
¼	cup olive oil
4	ounces fresh mushrooms
2	cups canned peeled tomatoes with their juice
⅓	cup tomato paste
1	teaspoon dried basil
½	teaspoon red pepper flakes
1	teaspoon salt
½	teaspoon fresh-ground black pepper

The filling

3	pounds fresh spinach
1	pound mozzarella cheese
1	cup (4 ounces) grated Parmesan cheese
½	pound fresh pasta dough
2	tablespoons salt
1	tablespoon olive oil

Prepare the sauce. Peel the onions, cut them in half lengthwise and slice very thin. Peel the garlic cloves and chop fine. Heat the oil in a large heavy saucepan and add the onions and garlic. Cook over medium heat, stirring occasionally, for 5 minutes. Wipe the mushrooms with a damp cloth or paper towel and trim tough ends from stems. Cut the mushrooms into thin slices. Add them to the saucepan and cook, stirring occasionally, for 3 minutes. Chop the tomatoes and add them with their juice, the tomato paste, basil, red pepper flakes, salt and pepper and mix well. Simmer, uncovered, over low heat for 40 minutes. Remove from heat and set aside until you are ready to assemble the lasagne.

Prepare the filling. Pick over spinach and discard any tough stems. Wash thoroughly in several changes of cold water and place in a very large stockpot. Cover and cook over high heat, in only the water that clings to the leaves, for 5 minutes. Remove the spinach to a colander and refresh under cold running water. Drain and squeeze out excess moisture. Fine-chop the spinach and reserve.

Slice the mozzarella very thin or use the shredding disk of a food processor.

Roll out pasta dough according to the step-by-step instructions and cut into lasagne strips. Bring 4 quarts of water to a boil and add the salt and oil. While the water is heating, lay a dampened towel on the work counter and set a bowl of cold water near the stove. Cook lasagne strips, a few at a time, for 15 to 20 seconds, plunge into cold water, then drain on the towel.

Preheat oven to 400°F.

Coat the inside of a baking dish with butter. Cover with a thin layer of sauce. Place a layer of pasta on the sauce; cover with a thin layer of chopped spinach and a layer of mozzarella cheese, then a layer of tomato sauce, topped by a sprinkling of Parmesan cheese. Continue making layers in the same way until all the ingredients are used, ending with a layer of pasta covered with Parmesan cheese.

Bake lasagne on center rack of oven for 15 minutes or until heated through. Let rest for 5 minutes before cutting into servings.

Chicken, Veal and Spinach Lasagne

6 to 8 portions

The filling

1	pound boneless, skinless chicken breasts	1	teaspoon fresh-grated nutmeg
1	pound boneless lean veal	1	teaspoon salt
2	large onions	1	teaspoon fresh-ground black pepper
4	tablespoons butter	8	ounces fresh mushrooms
¼	cup flour	1	pound fresh spinach
1¼	cups Chicken Stock (see Volume 1 Index) or canned broth	3	tablespoons heavy cream

2	cups Béchamel Sauce (see Volume 3 Index)	2	tablespoons salt
		1	tablespoon olive oil
1	pound fresh spinach pasta dough	1½	cups (6 ounces) grated Parmesan cheese

Prepare the filling. Cut the chicken breasts and veal into small cubes and put them through a meat grinder, or mince in a food processor. Peel the onions and chop fine. Melt the butter in a heavy, enameled saucepan. When the foam subsides, add the onions and cook, stirring occasionally, for 5 minutes. Add the ground chicken and veal and cook over medium heat, stirring occasionally, for 5 minutes longer, or until meat is lightly browned. Stir in the flour and, when it is well blended, beat in chicken stock, nutmeg, salt and pepper. Simmer, uncovered, for 30 minutes, stirring occasionally. Wipe the mushrooms with damp paper towels and slice them thin. Wash the spinach thoroughly, remove tough stalks, and chop fine. When the sauce has cooked for 30 minutes, add the mushrooms and spinach. Stir and let simmer, uncovered, 30 minutes more. Stir in the cream and remove mixture from heat.

Prepare the béchamel sauce.

Roll out the spinach pasta according to step-by-step instructions and cut into lasagne strips. Bring 4 quarts of water to a boil and add the salt and oil. While the water is heating, lay a dampened towel on the work counter and set a bowl of cold water near the stove. Cook lasagne strips, a few at a time, for 15 to 20 seconds, plunge into cold water, then drain on the towel.

Preheat the oven to 400°F.

Coat the inside of a baking pan with butter and spoon a small amount of sauce over it. Place a layer of lasagne strips on bottom of pan. Cover with a layer of filling, a layer of béchamel sauce and a layer of Parmesan cheese. Continue making alternate layers of pasta, filling, béchamel sauce and cheese, ending with a layer of pasta sprinkled liberally with Parmesan cheese.

Bake the lasagne on center rack of oven for 15 to 20 minutes, or until a knife inserted in the center for 10 seconds comes out hot to the touch. Let rest for 5 minutes before cutting into servings.

Cappelletti alla Panna

(Cappelletti in Cream Sauce)

4 portions

The filling

1	medium-size carrot
1	celery rib
2	tablespoons butter
2	ounces lean boneless pork
2	ounces lean boneless veal
2	ounces boiled ham
3	tablespoons medium-dry sherry or Marsala
1	large egg
½	cup (2 ounces) grated Parmesan cheese
	salt
	fresh-ground black pepper

½ pound fresh pasta dough

The sauce

1	cup heavy cream
½	cup fine-chopped fresh basil
2	tablespoons salt
1	tablespoon olive oil
	grated Parmesan cheese

Prepare the filling. Scrape and chop the carrot very fine. String celery, trim and chop fine. Melt the butter in a skillet and sauté carrot and celery over low heat for 5 minutes. Grind the pork, veal and ham together in a meat grinder or food processor and add to the vegetables in skillet. Sauté, stirring, until meat loses raw color. Add sherry or Marsala and, stirring occasionally, simmer gently, uncovered, for about 20 minutes, or until meat is cooked through and almost all the liquid has cooked away. Remove the mixture to a mixing bowl and stir in the egg, cheese, salt and freshly ground pepper to taste. Let cool completely before using.

Roll out pasta dough, cut into 2-inch squares, fill and shape following technique photos for Tortellini. Place the filled cappelletti on a well-floured cookie sheet and cover with a flour-dredged towel. Let cappelletti rest for 1 hour.

Prepare the sauce. Heat the cream in a small heavy saucepan and simmer together with basil until reduced by about one third. Pour into a heated bowl large enough to hold the cappelletti. Keep warm.

Bring 4 quarts of water to a boil, add salt and olive oil, and cook cappelletti for 5 minutes from when the water returns to a boil. Remove with a slotted spoon—letting them drain well—and place in the bowl with cream. Toss cappelletti with cream and serve with grated Parmesan cheese on the side.

Lasagne with Meat, Mushrooms, and Three Cheeses

6 to 8 portions

The sauce

2	large onions	1½	teaspoons salt
2	garlic cloves	1	teaspoon fresh-ground black pepper
¼	cup olive oil		
2	pounds lean ground beef	2	teaspoons sugar
4	cups canned peeled tomatoes with their juice	1	teaspoon dried basil
		2	bay leaves
½	cup tomato paste	8	ounces fresh mushrooms
½	cup water		

The cheeses

1	pound mozzarella cheese	1	cup (4 ounces) grated Parmesan cheese
1	pound ricotta cheese		

| 1 | pound fresh pasta dough | 1 | tablespoon olive oil |
| 2 | tablespoons salt | | |

Prepare the sauce. Peel the onions and garlic and chop fine. Heat the oil in a large heavy saucepan and add the onion and garlic. Cook, stirring, over medium heat for 5 minutes. Add the beef, breaking it up with a fork, and cook, stirring, for 5 minutes, or until meat is no longer pink. Drain tomatoes, reserving the juice, and chop them into rough pieces. Add them to the meat, along with the juice. Add tomato paste, water, salt, pepper, sugar, basil and bay leaves. Let sauce simmer, uncovered, for 2 hours, stirring occasionally.

After the sauce has simmered for 2 hours, wipe the mushrooms with a damp cloth or paper towels and trim tough ends from stems. Chop caps and stems and add to sauce. Let simmer for another hour. Remove from heat and reserve until you are ready to assemble the lasagne.

Cut the mozzarella cheese into thin slices or use the shredding disk of the food processor.

Roll out pasta dough according to step-by-step instructions, and cut into lasagne strips. Bring 4 quarts of water to a boil. While the water is heating, lay a dampened towel on the work counter and set a bowl of cold water near the stove. When the water has reached the boil, add the salt and the oil. Cook lasagne strips, a few at a time, for 15 to 20 seconds, plunge them into cold water, then drain on the towel.

Preheat oven to 400°F.

Coat the inside of a baking pan with butter. Skim any surface fat off the top of the sauce and discard. Spread a thin layer of sauce on the bottom of the pan. Arrange a layer of lasagne strips over the sauce; cover with a layer of meat sauce, and then with layers of ricotta, mozzarella and Parmesan cheese. Add another layer of pasta, then meat sauce and cheeses. Continue building alternate layers, ending with a layer of pasta covered liberally with Parmesan cheese.

Bake lasagne on center rack of oven for 15 to 20 minutes, or until a knife inserted in the center for 10 seconds comes out hot to the touch. Let rest for 5 minutes before cutting into servings.

Capri Ravioli

6 to 8 portions

The filling

6	ounces Parmesan cheese
8	ounces Gruyère cheese
2	large eggs
½	cup heavy cream
⅛	teaspoon fresh-grated nutmeg
1	tablespoon finely chopped fresh basil or parsley

1	pound fresh pasta dough
2	tablespoons salt
1	tablespoon olive oil
4	tablespoons butter
½	cup (2 ounces) grated Parmesan cheese
	or
2	cups Tomato Sauce (see Volume 4 Index)

Grate the cheeses for the filling and mix together in a bowl. Lightly beat the eggs and add them to the cheese, together with the cream, nutmeg and basil or parsley. Mix well and refrigerate until ready to use.

Roll out pasta dough and fill the ravioli following technique photos. Place them on a well-floured baking sheet as they are cut. Cover with a flour-dredged towel and let rest for 1 hour.

Bring 4 quarts water to a boil, add salt and olive oil, and cook ravioli for 5 minutes from when water returns to a boil. Remove with a slotted spoon to a warmed bowl.

Dress ravioli with butter and grated Parmesan cheese or with a homemade tomato sauce.

Cannelloni con Pollo e Prosciutto

(Homemade Cannelloni Filled with Chicken, Chicken Livers and Prosciutto)

4 portions

The filling		The sauce	
4	tablespoons butter	4	tablespoons butter
2	whole boneless chicken breasts	4	tablespoons flour
3	chicken livers	2½	cups milk
2	ounces prosciutto	½	cup heavy cream
¼	cup (1 ounce) grated Parmesan cheese	½	teaspoon salt
		¼	teaspoon fresh-ground white pepper
		⅛	teaspoon fresh-grated nutmeg
½	pound fresh pasta dough (see Index)	4	tablespoons unsalted butter
2	tablespoons salt	½	cup (2 ounces) grated Parmesan cheese
1	tablespoon olive oil		

Prepare the filling. Melt the 4 tablespoons butter in a heavy skillet. Add chicken breasts and sauté over medium heat for 3 minutes on each side. Remove them with a slotted spoon and reserve. Add the chicken livers and, still over medium heat, sauté for about 2 minutes on each side. Put the chicken breasts, chicken livers and prosciutto through a meat grinder or cut into smaller pieces and mince together in a food processor. Mix well with ¼ cup grated Parmesan cheese and refrigerate until needed.

To make the sauce, melt the 4 tablespoons of butter in a medium-size saucepan, add the flour and cook over low heat, stirring with a wooden spoon, for 2 to 3 minutes. Heat the milk and cream in another saucepan until hot but not boiling. Remove roux from heat and, stirring constantly with a wire whisk, add hot milk all at once. Return to heat, stir in salt, pepper and nutmeg and cook, stirring frequently with a wire whisk, for 5 to 10 minutes. Remove from heat and add ¾ cup of sauce to the filling mixture. Mix well, and return to

refrigerator. Coat remaining sauce with a film of butter and reserve.

Roll out pasta dough according to step-by-step instructions and cut into rectangles for cannelloni. Bring 4 quarts of water to a boil. While the water is heating, lay a dampened towel on the work counter and set a bowl of cold water near the stove. When the water has come to a boil, add the oil and salt. Cook the cannelloni strips, a few at a time, for 15 to 20 seconds, plunge into cold water, then lay out to drain on the towel.

Preheat oven to 400°F. Coat a large ovenproof baking dish with approximately 1 tablespoon of the butter and set aside.

Place 2 tablespoons of filling on each pasta rectangle and roll like a crêpe. Arrange filled cannelloni seam side down in the buttered baking dish. Spread the sauce over the cannelloni, sprinkle with ½ cup Parmesan cheese and dot with remaining butter. Bake on center rack of oven for 15 to 20 minutes, or until lightly browned.

Four-Cheese Ravioli Filling

for 1 pound fresh pasta dough

4	ounces Parmesan cheese	½	cup heavy cream
2	ounces Romano cheese	2	tablespoons fine-chopped parsley
4	ounces Gruyère or Emmentaler cheese		several grindings of black pepper
8	ounces ricotta cheese		
1	large egg		

Grate the Parmesan, Romano and Gruyère or Emmentaler cheeses and mix together with ricotta cheese in a medium-size bowl. Beat egg lightly and add to cheeses, together with

cream, parsley and freshly ground black pepper to taste. Mix well, let cool and refrigerate until ready to use.

Cannelloni with Ground Beef and Spinach

4 portions

The filling

1	small onion
2	garlic cloves
1½	tablespoons olive oil
1	tablespoon butter
8	ounces lean ground beef
8	ounces fresh spinach
¼	cup (1 ounce) grated Parmesan cheese
1½	tablespoons heavy cream
1	egg
½	teaspoon dried orégano
¼	teaspoon salt
¼	teaspoon fresh-ground black pepper

½	pound fresh pasta dough
2	tablespoons salt
1	tablespoon olive oil

2	tablespoons unsalted butter
¾	cup (3 ounces) grated Parmesan cheese

The tomato sauce

1	small onion
2	tablespoons olive oil
2	cups canned peeled tomatoes, with their juice
⅓	cup tomato paste
½	teaspoon dried basil
½	teaspoon dried orégano
1	teaspoon sugar
½	teaspoon salt
¼	teaspoon fresh-ground black pepper

The cream sauce

2	tablespoons butter
4	tablespoons flour
½	cup plus 2 tablespoons milk
3	tablespoons heavy cream
¼	teaspoon salt
⅛	teaspoon fresh-ground white pepper

Prepare the filling. Peel the onion and garlic and chop fine. Heat the oil and butter in a large skillet. Cook the onion and garlic over medium heat for 5 minutes. Add the meat, breaking it up with a fork, and cook, stirring occasionally, for 10 minutes, or until meat is brown. While meat is cooking, wash spinach thoroughly and trim. Place in a large covered pot and cook for 10 minutes in just the water clinging to the leaves. Refresh under cold running water and squeeze out excess moisture. Chop fine and add to the meat mixture. Cook, stirring, for 3 or 4 minutes, or until all the moisture has evaporated. Transfer mixture to a medium-size bowl. Add Parmesan and heavy cream. Break the egg into a cup, beat lightly with a fork, and add to meat-spinach mixture. Add orégano, salt and pepper and mix well. Refrigerate until ready to stuff the cannelloni.

Prepare the tomato sauce. Peel the onion and chop it fine. Heat the olive oil in a heavy saucepan. Add the onion and cook for 5 minutes over moderate heat. Chop tomatoes and add them with their juice to the saucepan. Add tomato paste, basil, orégano, sugar, salt and pepper. Simmer over low heat for 40 minutes, stirring occasionally. Remove from heat and set aside.

Prepare the cream sauce. Melt the butter in a small heavy saucepan over medium heat. Stir in the flour and cook, stirring, for 2 minutes. Heat ½ cup milk together with the heavy cream until hot but not boiling. Remove butter-flour mixture from heat and, stirring constantly, pour in the hot liquid all at once. Continue to stir until well blended and smooth. Return to medium heat, and cook, stirring constantly, until sauce comes to a boil. Remove from heat and add salt and pepper. The sauce will be very thick. Pour the 2 tablespoons of milk over the top of the sauce to prevent a skin from forming and set the sauce aside.

Roll out the pasta dough according to step-by-step instructions and cut into strips for cannelloni. Bring 4 quarts of water to a boil. While the water is heating, lay a dampened towel on the work counter and set a bowl of cold water near the stove. When the water is at a boil, add salt and oil. Cook the cannelloni strips, a few at a time, for 15 to 20 seconds, plunge into the cold water, then drain on the towel.

Preheat oven to 400°F. Coat a large ovenproof baking dish with 1 tablespoon butter. Place 2 tablespoons filling on each pasta rectangle and roll like a crêpe. Spread a thin layer of tomato sauce in the bottom of the baking dish and arrange the cannelloni side by side, seam side down. Stir the milk into the cream sauce and spoon over cannelloni. Pour the remaining tomato sauce over the top. Sprinkle with Parmesan cheese and dot with remaining butter. Bake for 15 to 20 minutes, or until lightly browned.

Tortellini Verde al Pesto

(Spinach Tortellini with Basil Sauce)

4 portions

The filling	
1	small chicken breast
2	ounces lean boneless pork
2	tablespoons butter
1	lemon
1	tablespoon grated Parmesan cheese
1	egg
½	teaspoon fresh-grated nutmeg
	salt
	fresh-ground black pepper

½   pound fresh spinach pasta dough

2   cups Pesto (see Volume 4 Index)

2   tablespoons salt
1   tablespoon olive oil
     grated Parmesan cheese

Prepare the filling. Slice chicken breast and pork into thin strips. Heat butter in large skillet until it foams. When foam subsides, add chicken strips and cook, stirring, for approximately 3 minutes. Remove to bowl of food processor or blender. Add pork strips and cook over medium-high heat, stirring, for 5 minutes. Remove to bowl of food processor or blender. Grate the rind of the lemon to measure ¼ teaspoon. Add the cheese, egg, lemon rind, nutmeg, salt and pepper to the meats. Process or blend until meat is ground and everything is well mixed. Refrigerate.

Roll out pasta dough, cut out circles with a 2-inch cookie cutter, fill and shape following technique photos for Tortellini. Place on a well-floured cookie sheet and cover with a flour-dredged towel. Let rest for 1 hour.

Heat the Pesto.

Bring 4 quarts of water to a boil. Add the salt and olive oil. Cook tortellini for 5 minutes from when water returns to a boil. While tortellini are cooking, beat 1 or 2 tablespoons of tortellini cooking water into the pesto. Drain tortellini, place in large bowl, and toss with pesto sauce. Serve immediately. Pass extra grated Parmesan cheese.

Ravioli de Rapallo

(Ravioli Filled with Spinach and Cheese in a Walnut Sauce)

6 to 8 portions

The filling

2	eggs
1	10-ounce package fresh spinach
4	tablespoons unsalted butter
¾	cup ricotta cheese
¼	teaspoon fresh-grated nutmeg
¼	teaspoon salt
¼	teaspoon fresh-ground white pepper

The sauce

2	ounces pecorino cheese, such as Romano
1	cup shelled walnuts
½	cup shelled cashew nuts
½	cup ricotta cheese
½	cup milk
6	tablespoons heavy cream
3	tablespoons olive oil
1	tablespoon water
1	pound fresh pasta dough
2	tablespoons salt
1	tablespoon olive oil

Prepare the filling. Hard-cook the eggs, peel and chop. Wash spinach thoroughly and trim tough stems. Heat butter in a skillet. When foam subsides add spinach and cook, stirring, for 4 minutes. Place spinach, chopped eggs, ricotta cheese, nutmeg, salt and pepper in bowl of food processor or blender and process or blend to a coarse purée. Remove to a small mixing bowl, let cool and refrigerate until needed.

Prepare the sauce. Grate the pecorino cheese in a food processor or blender. Chop the nuts slightly and then turn into processor or blender. Process until nuts are pulverized and then mix with cheese. Add ricotta, milk, cream, olive oil and water. Process until sauce is well mixed and has a creamy texture.

Roll out pasta dough and fill the ravioli according to technique photos. Place them on a well-floured baking sheet as they are cut. Cover with a flour-dredged towel and let rest for 1 hour.

Bring 4 quarts water to a boil, add the salt and olive oil, and cook ravioli for 5 minutes from when water returns to a boil. Remove cooked ravioli with a slotted spoon and place in a warmed bowl. While the ravioli are cooking, heat the walnut sauce. Pour over drained ravioli. Toss gently and serve immediately.

Chicken Filling for Ravioli, Tortellini and Cappelletti

for 1 pound fresh pasta dough

3	boneless, skinless chicken breasts	2	large eggs	
1	Bouquet Garni (see Volume 1 Index)	1/8	teaspoon fresh-grated nutmeg	
1	lemon		salt	
1/2	cup (2 ounces) grated Parmesan cheese		fresh-ground black pepper	

Place chicken breasts in a small saucepan and add just enough water to cover. Add the *bouquet garni*. Bring chicken to a simmer and poach for 30 minutes. Remove chicken breasts and reserve poaching liquid to make stock or soup. Cut chicken breasts into pieces and place in bowl of food processor. Grate the rind of the lemon to measure 1/2 tea-spoon. Add cheese, eggs, lemon rind and nutmeg to chicken and process until smooth. Add salt and pepper to taste. Or chop chicken very fine and then combine with remaining ingredients. If mixture is too dry, add a teaspoon or two of the poaching liquid. Mix well. Let cool and refrigerate until needed.

Sausage and Meat Tortellini in Spicy Tomato Sauce

6 to 8 portions

The filling

4	ounces mortadella, or Polish kielbasa sausage
2	ounces prosciutto
2	ounces lean boneless veal
2	ounces lean boneless pork
2	tablespoons butter
¼	cup bread crumbs
¼	cup finely chopped parsley
	salt
	fresh-ground black pepper
1	pound fresh pasta dough

The sauce

1	small onion
1	garlic clove
1	celery rib
2	tablespoons olive oil
4	cups canned peeled tomatoes with their juice
1	teaspoon dried orégano
¼	cup dry red wine
	salt
	fresh-ground black pepper
2	tablespoons salt
1	tablespoon olive oil
	grated Parmesan cheese

Prepare the filling. Put the mortadella, prosciutto, veal and pork through a meat grinder, or chop fine in a food processor. Heat the butter in a heavy skillet and add the meats. Cook, stirring, over high heat for 8 to 10 minutes, until thoroughly cooked. Remove to a mixing bowl and add bread crumbs and parsley. Stir in salt and pepper to taste. Let cool and refrigerate until needed.

Roll out pasta dough, cut out circles with 2-inch cookie cutter, and fill and shape according to instructions for tortellini. Place on a well-floured cookie sheet and cover with a flour-dredged towel. Let rest for 1 hour.

Prepare the sauce. Peel the onion and garlic and chop fine. String celery, trim and chop fine. Heat the olive oil in a deep skillet or heavy saucepan. Add onion, celery and garlic and sauté for 5 to 6 minutes, stirring frequently. Drain the tomatoes and rough-chop them. Discard juice or reserve for another use. Add them to the other vegetables along with the orégano and wine. Simmer for 40 minutes, stirring occasionally. Season with salt and pepper to taste.

Bring 4 quarts of water to a boil, add salt and olive oil, and drop in tortellini. Cook for 5 minutes from when water returns to a boil. Drain and place in warmed serving dish. Pour the sauce over the tortellini and serve immediately with grated Parmesan cheese.

Ravioli Piedmontese

(Ravioli Filled with Beef and Tomatoes)

6 to 8 portions

The filling

1	large onion
1	garlic clove
4	tablespoons butter
1	tablespoon vegetable oil
12	ounces lean ground beef
1	cup Beef Stock (see Volume 1 Index) or canned broth
1	pound fresh pasta dough
2	tablespoons salt
1	tablespoon olive oil

1	cup canned peeled tomatoes with their juice
1	teaspoon dried rosemary
½	teaspoon dried basil
	salt
	fresh-ground black pepper
2	eggs
½	cup (2 ounces) grated Parmesan cheese
	grated Parmesan cheese

Prepare the filling. Peel the onion and garlic and chop fine. Heat butter and oil in heavy saucepan. When foam subsides, add the onion and garlic and cook, stirring occasionally, for 8 to 10 minutes. Add the beef and break apart with a fork. Cook, stirring occasionally, until meat has browned. Pour in stock. Chop tomatoes and add them to the saucepan together with their juice. Grind rosemary in a mortar. Add rosemary and basil to meat mixture. Stir and cook over medium heat for about 15 minutes. Season to taste with salt and pepper. Remove from heat and strain contents through a fine sieve held over a small saucepan. Set liquid aside. Put the solid ingredients in a mixing bowl. Beat eggs lightly. Add Parmesan cheese and eggs to mixing bowl. Mix well, let cool, and refrigerate until ready to use.

Roll out pasta dough and fill ravioli according to technique photos. Place them on a well-floured baking sheet as they are cut. Cover with a flour-dredged towel and let rest for 1 hour.

Bring 4 quarts water to a boil, add the salt and olive oil, and cook ravioli for 5 minutes after water returns to a boil. Remove with a slotted spoon to a warmed bowl.

While the ravioli are cooking, heat the reserved beef-cooking liquid. Drain ravioli, remove to a warmed serving dish, and pour the cooking liquid over them. Serve immediately with extra grated Parmesan cheese.

Part Four
CHEESECAKES

Today's lovers of cheesecake may be surprised to discover that this delicacy, in one form or another, appears throughout most of recorded culinary history, with the earliest surviving recipes dating to the first cookbooks of ancient Greece. That shouldn't be surprising, however, when you consider that milk, honey and cheese were staples of the Athenian army in early campaigns. Wherever in history those ingredients have been in good supply, cheesecake was soon to follow.

Cheesecake was celebrated by the Greeks in verse and song, and in the third century A.D. an Alexandrian Greek named Athenaeus devoted an entire section of his gastronomical treatise, *The Deipnosophists,* to the subject. In it he described a great number of the cheesecakes that were the specialties of every Greek province and city state. Some were as simple as a mold of freshly made cheese sweetened with honey and chilled in the snow. Others were more elaborate pastries in which cheese was mixed with eggs and other ingredients and baked. One variation even called for the cake to be molded in the shape of a woman's breast.

Cheesecake was used as a ritual offering to the gods, and was given as a reward to the man who could stay awake the longest in pan-Hellenic games. History has even taken the trouble to note that Xanthippe, the notoriously ill-tempered wife of Socrates, once snatched from his hands and destroyed a delicacy sent to the great man by one of his admirers. The delicacy, of course, was cheesecake.

With the rise of the Roman empire, cheesecake made its way to Italy, where it has been a favorite ever since. The Roman philosopher Cato, who was also one of the outstanding cooks of his day, recorded several recipes for cheesecake. One of them is reproduced in Barbara Norman's *Tales of the Table*: "Bray 2 lbs. of cheese thoroughly in a mortar; when it is thoroughly macerated, add 1 pound of wheat flour, or, if you wish the cake to be more dainty, ½ lb. of fine flour, and mix thoroughly with the cheese. Add 1 egg, and work the whole well. Pat out a loaf, place on leaves, and bake slowly on a warm hearth under a crock. —Cato, *De Agricultura,* Book LXXV."

A more elaborate version for a cake called *Torta di Ricotta,* which calls for many egg yolks, beaten egg whites, orange and lemon rind, brandy, currants, pine nuts and cinnamon, appeared in Bartolomeo Stefani's *L'Arte di ben cucinare,* c. 1662. To this day Italians enjoy a vast number of sweet pastries that are based on a rich mixture of sweetened ricotta cheese, usually heavily spiced with cinnamon, cloves and nutmeg.

Perhaps the Romans introduced the cheesecake to Western Europe and Great Britain in particular, where it flourished and became a popular traditional dish by the seventeenth century. Samuel Pepys wrote in his diary on August 11, 1667, about "some of the best cheesecakes that ever I [ate] in my life." And Anne Boleyn is said to have attempted to gain King Henry VIII's heart by inventing the small, delicate cheesecakes known as Maids of Honour.

In eighteenth-century Britain almost all open tarts were filled with a mixture of heavy cream and egg yolks to which the juice of lemons or oranges or a purée of fruits or berries was added. The acid of the fruit juice or purée curdled the cream and turned these tarts into cheesecakes. These may well have marked the beginnings of our own tradition of adding elaborate fruit toppings to the basic cheesecake.

Oddly, France never developed a repertory of cheesecake recipes, although with characteristic Gallic elegance and simplicity they have contributed the lovely dessert called *Coeur à la Crème.* A rich cream cheese is pressed and shaped in heart-shaped molds and served in single portions traditionally—though not always—garnished with sugared strawberries.

In Russia, cheesecake is called *paskha* and became an Easter tradition of the Orthodox Church. In fact, in the Russian language, the word *"paskha"* (related to our word "Paschal") actually means Easter as well as referring to this special cake, which is eaten only then. It is a very rich confection of very fresh soft cheese—farmer cheese, pot cheese or cottage cheese—combined with quantities of butter, eggs, sugar and vanilla. *Paskha* used to be made in special wooden molds in the shape of a truncated pyramid with the Cyrillic letters XB on the side. The letters stand for "Christos Voskres"—Christ is Risen—and indeed, the renewed availability of dairy products in the spring is part of the symbolic resurrection that Easter celebrates.

If it is true that cheesecake has ancient and foreign origins, it is also true that the form of cheesecake most common in America today owes its chief ingredient to a fairly recent and distinctly domestic development. It was just over a hundred years ago (in 1872) that American dairymen, looking to compete with the popular French cheese, *neufchâtel,* came up with a little something they called cream cheese. Cheesecake was never the same again.

If we have come to think of cheesecake as something rich and slightly sinful, it is not surprising that the word has been borrowed to denote a certain kind of mildly risqué photography. One story has it that in 1922 one James Kane, a New York *Journal* photographer and presumably a great fancier of cheese pastry, expressed his enthusiasm for a perfectly exposed photograph of a somewhat unexpectedly over-exposed young actress by exclaiming, "That's real cheesecake!" *The Morris Dictionary of Word and Phrase Origins* suggests that the old-time photographer's refrain, "say cheese," and the turn-of-the-century currency of terms for attractive females like "cupcake," "cookie," or "babycakes" may have linguistically melded to create a tasty new term for racy photographs.

CHEESE-CAKES

This popular cake probably originated in Greece and is now world famous. There are hundreds of variations, but the basic ingredients are similar: cottage, curd, or cream cheese, eggs, and a thickening agent such as flour, cornstarch or ground nuts. Extra ingredients are added for flavor, fresh or dried fruits, extracts and spices being the most common.

Cheesecake Bases

Cheesecake usually has a firm base. This is put into the pan before the filling or spread over the top of the filling; in the latter case, the cake is inverted before serving. The purpose of the base is to provide a textural and flavor contrast and to enable you to cut and serve the cheesecake with ease. There are several types of bases to choose from.

Cracker or Cookie Crumbs. Crushed crackers or cookies combined with melted butter make a crunchy crust and are a traditional base for cheesecakes. The amount of crumbs used will depend on how thick a crust you want—1 to 1½ cups is the usual amount for an 8- to 9-inch base.

Plain crumbly cookies or crackers are the best ones to use as they make good crumbs and readily absorb the binding ingredients. Graham crackers, gingersnaps, chocolate wafers, shortbread and vanilla wafers are all good choices. Avoid using close-textured cookies; they reduce to a fine powder instead of crumbs.

Cereals. Cornflakes, bran flakes, rolled oats and puffed cereals can also be used. Do not use sugar- or honey-coated cereals as they will not stick together.

To prepare the pan for a crumb crust, lightly coat it with fat so that the crumbs will adhere. For a bottom crust, add the crumbs to the pan and use your fingers to press the crumbs into a crust. For a really solid base, press down on the crumbs with a spoon, the base of a pie plate or a glass jar. Although this crust sometimes is baked, it can be used unbaked as well. For refrigerator cheesecakes, the base is simply chilled for 30 minutes or so to set the butter. If chocolate is used as part of the binding ingredients, the setting time will be several hours.

Short-Crust Pastry. Pastry is often used for traditional European cheesecakes such as *Crostata di Ricotta* and Yorkshire Cheesecakes. A rich short-crust pastry (see Volume 2 Index) is excellent. If the pastry is to be used as a base, and not to line the pan, roll it out to the diameter of the pan. Use a rolling pin to lift the pastry into the pan. Press the pastry tight against the circumference of the pan so that it fits snugly; trim the edges of the pastry if necessary. Prick the crust all over with a fork. Bake in a preheated 400°F oven for 15 minutes. This will crisp the pastry and prevent the filling from soaking into it and making a soggy crust.

Individual recipes will state the amount of pastry needed for the crust. This will vary depending on whether it is used as a base, or to line the pan, or in some cases to make a lattice on top of the filling.

Sponge Mixture. Some Eastern European cheesecakes use a sponge cake as the base. The cake is a simple mixture of all-purpose flour, baking

Making a Crumb Crust

1 Butter base and sides of loose-bottomed or springform cake or tart pan. Break cookies into pieces and place in heavy plastic bag.

2 Squeeze air from bag and seal. Crush cookies by pressing down firmly with rolling pin. Or break cookies and spin in blender or processor.

3 If necessary, put crumbs through coarse sieve into bowl or onto a sheet of wax paper to separate them. Melt butter and remove from heat.

powder, butter, sugar and egg. The sponge is usually not baked before the filling is added. The only exception to this is in the *Cassata alla Siciliana* and other cakes like it, where the sponge is baked separately and an uncooked cheese mixture is sandwiched between the layers.

Flavorings. Although not essential, an extra bit of flavor is a nice addition to a crumb crust. A teaspoon of powdered cinnamon, ginger, nutmeg or other spice can be added without any adjustment in ingredients. Other ingredients such as finely chopped or ground nuts, shredded coconut, or finely chopped dried fruit should be used as a replacement for part of the dry ingredients: Subtract 2 tablespoons of the dry ingredients and replace with 2 tablespoons of the flavoring ingredient.

Binding Ingredients. In order to make the crumbs stick together and form a crust, they must be mixed with a liquid that hardens on setting. The most commonly used binding agent is melted butter. The butter should be cut into small pieces and set to melt over low heat in a small heavy-gauge saucepan. Watch the butter carefully so that it does not brown. If sugar is used in the recipe, it is added to the hot, melted butter. Butter can also be used in combination with other liquid flavorings or sweeteners such as molasses, honey or melted chocolate. For the first two, the total amount of binding remains the same but one third of the quantity of butter is replaced with honey or molasses. For chocolate, however, the replacement ratio changes because chocolate has a variable fat content. Whether chocolate, molasses or honey, heat together with the butter.

Equipment

When a cheesecake is to be free-standing, a springform or loose-bottomed pan is essential because both are constructed so they can be removed from the cake rather than the cake removed from them—important when the cake is as easily bruised as is cheesecake. Otherwise, very little special equipment is needed for making cheesecakes.

Filling Ingredients

The filling for a cheesecake can be dense and firm and baked in the oven, or light and airy and set in the refrigerator. Results will vary tremendously depending on the ingredients you use and whether the cheesecake is baked. There are, however, some common ingredients.

Cheese. When making a cheese-cake, there are four basic kinds of cheese to choose from. Cream cheese is available in a variety of styles: full fat (often available at delicatessens and cheese stores), Philadelphia, and low fat. Whipped cream cheeses are not as satisfactory for baking. Farmer cheese, a simple fresh thick cheese pressed before packaging, has a low moisture content. Ricotta, similar to farmer cheese but creamier, gives a grainier texture to a finished cake than cream cheese. Pot cheese is a mild dry cheese with curds; cottage cheese, which is similar to pot cheese, has a greater moisture content than any of the other cheeses.

Butter. Butter enriches the filling and keeps it moist. Usually a small amount is used. Incorporate it into the filling either by beating it with the sugar or by melting it and beating it in.

Eggs. Eggs are added to refrigerator cheesecakes to add richness

4 Add sugar and flavorings to crumbs. Add crumbs to butter; mix until crumbs cling together when pressed. Scatter ¼-inch layer of crumbs over base of pan.

5 Press crumbs in place with the back of a spoon or bottom of pie plate. Tilt pan toward you; put 2 spoonfuls of crumbs on the section nearest you. Press in place.

6 Continue until the circumference of the pan is covered. Even out the crust by pressing a smooth-sided jar around the inside of the ring.

Lemon Cheesecake

8 portions

The base

½	cup all-purpose flour
½	teaspoon baking powder
4	tablespoons unsalted butter, at room temperature
¼	cup sugar
1	egg

The filling

1	pound cottage cheese
2	eggs
1	lemon
⅓	cup sugar
3	tablespoons cornstarch
⅔	cup heavy cream
¼	cup golden raisins

The topping

⅔	cup sour cream	1	tablespoon sugar

1 Sift flour and baking powder together. Combine ingredients for base in a mixing bowl. Beat about 3 minutes, until mixture is of soft dropping consistency.

3 Spread the base mixture onto the bottom of prepared pan. Smooth the top with a spatula so that the layer is even.

4 Push the cottage cheese through a sieve into a bowl. Beat the eggs lightly, and gradually beat into the cheese.

5 Grate rind and squeeze juice from lemon into cheese mixture. Add remaining ingredients for filling to cheese and egg mixture. Beat until well blended.

7 Combine the sour cream and sugar for the topping in a small bowl.

8 After 30 minutes, spoon the topping over the cake. Return to oven for 5 minutes. Turn off oven and leave cheesecake in oven until cool.

9 To remove from pan, release clip at side. Run an icing spatula around sides to loosen. Lift away sides. Run spatula across bottom to loosen.

Topping Cheesecake

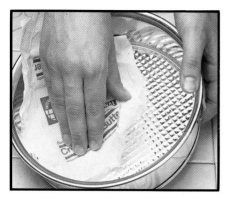

2 Lightly butter an 8-inch spring-form cake pan. Preheat oven to 350°F.

1 For grape topping, halve, if necessary, seed and if desired skin grapes. Arrange in circles on the cheesecake.

2 Fresh fruit such as pitted tangerines, strawberries, or a mixture of colorful fruit may be used in the same manner as grapes.

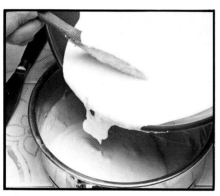

6 Spoon the cheese mixture over the base. Smooth and level with a spatula. Bake in the middle level of oven for 30 minutes.

3 Glaze fresh fruit with melted redcurrant, apple or apricot jelly thinned with a small amount of water. Pour over fruit.

4 Canned fruit may be used in the same manner as fresh. Drain well, saving the juice to thicken for glaze.

10 Lift cake off bottom of pan, using a metal spatula. Carefully transfer to a serving plate. Serve cut into wedges.

5 Measure juice. Add 2 teaspoons arrowroot for every ⅔ cup juice. Bring to simmer over low heat. Simmer 1 minute. Cool. Pour over fruit.

6 For sour cream topping, spoon cream over cake about 5 minutes before end of cooking time and return cake to oven to set cream.

and to baked cheesecakes to set the filling. In unbaked cheesecakes, the eggs are often separated and the yolks and whites incorporated separately. All of these recipes are based on the use of large eggs.

Sugar. Sugar is used as a sweetener and to add smoothness to the texture of the cake.

Cream and Yogurt. Heavy cream, sour cream and yogurt are often added to the filling of both refrigerator and baked cheesecakes. Sour cream is also used as a topping.

Flavorings. Extracts, spices, grated citrus rinds and juices are popular flavorings in both refrigerator and baked cheesecakes. Amounts may be varied to suit your taste.

Fruit. Raw or cooked fruit (depending on type) can be spread over the base of the cheesecake before the filling is added, mixed with the filling, or used as a topping (see Index). Fruits that can be used raw include strawberries, raspberries, blueberries, blackberries, pineapple, mangos, kiwis, and pitted tangerines. Plums, pears, peaches, nectarines and apricots can be used raw or poached. Apples, rhubarb, gooseberries, cranberries or dried fruit can be used stewed. Well-drained canned fruits such as pears, apricots, peaches or pineapple, cherries, mandarin oranges, or plums can also be used.

Stabilizers. In some baked cakes a stabilizer such as ground almonds, cornstarch, or flour is added to the filling to absorb moisture during cooking. Cakes with a stabilizer added usually have a firm texture. Unbaked cheesecakes also need a stabilizer to set the ingredients, so powdered gelatin dissolved in water or fruit juice is stirred into the filling. The amount of gelatin varies with the type of cheese and amount of liquid in the filling. Do not be tempted to add a bit extra "just in case"—too much gelatin gives a rubbery, tough result. Always let the dissolved gelatin cool before adding, and always add it gradually, stirring constantly as you pour it in a thin stream.

Cassata alla Siciliana

This Italian cheesecake is based on a whisked spongecake. Ricotta cheese is the choice in Italy, but sieved cottage cheese can be used as a substitute.

12 portions

1	Whole-Egg Spongecake (see Volume 8 Index), baked in an 8-inch springform pan		**The filling**
		1½	pounds ricotta or cottage cheese
		¼	cup sugar
		2	ounces semisweet chocolate
		½	teaspoon almond extract

The icing

1	egg white	2	teaspoons lemon juice
1½	cups confectioners' sugar	4	ounces glacéed fruit

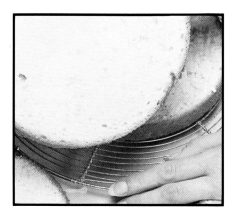

1 Split the cake into three equal layers, using a sharp serrated knife.

2 Push the cheese through a sieve into a bowl. Beat in the sugar. Coarsely grate the chocolate and beat in.

3 Beat in the almond extract. Divide the mixture in half. Spread one half over one of the sponge layers.

4 Top with second sponge layer and spread layer with remaining cheese mixture. Top with third sponge layer.

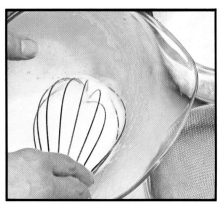

5 Lightly whisk the egg white until stiff but not dry (see Volume 9 Index). Sift the confectioners' sugar.

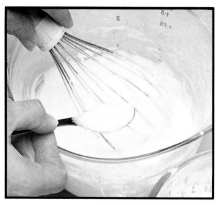

6 A tablespoon at a time, whisk half of the confectioners' sugar into the egg white.

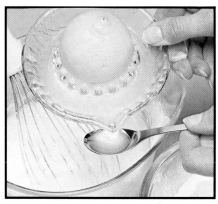

7 Stir in the lemon juice. Continue adding confectioners' sugar until mixture reaches a coating consistency.

8 Spread the icing over the top and sides of cake, using icing spatula.

9 Decorate the cake with the glacéed fruit. Leave in a cool place or refrigerate to set for about 1 hour.

Zwieback Refrigerator Cheesecake

Zwieback means twice baked in German, and is the name given to a rusklike sweet bread. This refrigerator cheesecake has a zwieback base and a very creamy filling. Without the topping, it freezes well—allow to thaw at room temperature for at least 3 hours.

8 portions

The base

14	zwieback rusks
6	tablespoons unsalted butter
½	teaspoon ground allspice

The topping

8	ounces raspberries or blackberries

The filling

¼	cup water
2	envelopes gelatin (2 scant tablespoons)
3	eggs
⅓	cup sugar
1	pound cream cheese, at room temperature
1	lemon
2	cups sour cream
½	teaspoon vanilla extract

Crush the zwieback between pieces of wax paper. Melt the butter in a small saucepan over low heat. Add the crumbs and allspice. Stir until the mixture is well combined and clings together. Butter pan. Press the crumbs into the bottom of an 8-inch round loose-bottomed cake pan. Cover and refrigerate for 30 minutes, or until set.

Put water in a small saucepan; sprinkle on the gelatin. Let stand 5 minutes. Set over very low heat until the gelatin becomes liquid, about 3 minutes. Cool slightly.

Separate the eggs, reserving the whites for another use. In a medium-size bowl, beat the yolks and sugar together until light, fluffy and lemon-colored. Remove the pan from the heat and stir in the dissolved gelatin. Place cream cheese in a large bowl; beat until smooth and creamy. Gradually beat in the egg mixture, stirring constantly to break up any lumps. Grate the rind from the lemon; add to the cheese mixture along with the sour cream and vanilla extract. Stir to blend thoroughly. Spoon the mixture into the prepared crust, smoothing the top with a spatula. Cover the cake and refrigerate 2 to 3 hours, or until the cheese mixture is set.

One half hour before serving, gently wash berries and spread out on paper towels to dry.

When ready to serve, if necessary, loosen the cake from sides of pan by easing an icing spatula or knife between the inside of the pan and the crust and moving it carefully around the circumference of the pan; lift out the cake and transfer to a serving plate. Arrange the berries over the top and serve.

Semolina-Almond Cheesecake with Cherry Topping

The rich pastry crust on this cheesecake must be baked first so that it will not become soggy.

8 to 10 portions

1	recipe rich Short-Crust Pastry (see Volume 2 Index)

The topping

1	pound canned black cherries in syrup
1	tablespoon arrowroot

The filling

4	tablespoons unsalted butter
⅓	cup sugar
2	eggs
8	ounces cottage cheese
⅓	cup (2 ounces) blanched almonds
	few drops of almond extract
2	tablespoons semolina flour

Preheat the oven to 400°F. Roll out the pastry to fit the bottom and sides of an 8-inch springform pan. Prick the base of the pastry; line with foil or parchment and add weights, such as dry beans, for baking blind. Bake for 15 minutes.

Remove pastry from oven. Remove foil and weights. Cream the butter and sugar in a large bowl until light and fluffy. Separate the eggs; place the whites in a large bowl, and one by one, beat the yolks into the butter mixture. Press the cottage cheese through a sieve into the butter mixture; beat until smooth. Grind the almonds and add to the mixture along with the almond extract and semolina. Stir until blended. Whisk the egg whites until stiff but not dry (see Volume 9 Index). Stir one quarter of the whites into the cheese mixture, then fold in the rest. Gently spoon the mix-

ture into the crust and smooth with a spatula. Bake on a rack in the middle level of the oven for 45 minutes. Turn off the oven and leave cheesecake in oven until cool. If necessary, use an icing spatula to loosen cheesecake from sides of pan; release clip and remove cake. Transfer cheesecake to serving plate.

Drain the cherries, reserving ¾ cup of the syrup. In small saucepan, make a glaze by blending the arrowroot with 2 tablespoons of the reserved syrup. Add rest of the syrup and bring to a boil; simmer 1 minute over medium heat. Cool slightly. Arrange the drained cherries on top of the cake and spoon the cooled glaze over them. Let glaze set. Serve the cake cut into wedges.

Pineapple-Ricotta Cheesecake

12 portions

The base

8	ounces shortbread cookies	2	tablespoons sugar
4	ounces plus 1 teaspoon unsalted butter	½	teaspoon ground allspice

The filling

3	eggs	2	tablespoons all-purpose flour
1	large ripe pineapple		
2½	pounds ricotta cheese	½	teaspoon vanilla extract
1	lemon	⅛	teaspoon ground allspice
¼	cup sugar	8	walnut halves

Preheat the oven to 350°F. Crush the cookies between pieces of wax paper. Coat a 9-inch round loose-bottomed cake pan with the 1 teaspoon butter. Melt the remaining butter in a small saucepan over low heat. Add crumbs, sugar and allspice; stir until the mixture is well combined and the crumbs cling together. Press the mixture evenly into the bottom of the prepared pan; set aside.

Separate the eggs, reserving the whites for another purpose. Peel and core the pineapple. Chop the fruit very fine; set aside. Put the ricotta through a wire-mesh sieve into a medium-size bowl. Grate the rind from the lemon. Add it to the cheese along with the sugar, flour, vanilla and allspice. Beat until the mixture is well blended. Add the egg yolks, one at a time, beating until well combined.

Spoon half the mixture into the prepared pan; smooth with a spatula. Spread the chopped pineapple evenly over the filling. Spoon the remaining ricotta filling over the pineapple and smooth it with a metal spatula so that it covers the pineapple completely. Bake on a rack in the middle level of the oven for 20 minutes. Remove the cheesecake from the oven and arrange the walnuts decoratively on top. Return the cheesecake to the oven and bake for another 10 to 15 minutes, or until the filling is firm. Turn off oven and leave cheesecake in oven until cool. If necessary, use an icing spatula to loosen the cheesecake from the sides of pan; remove cake from pan. Carefully transfer cheesecake to serving plate. Cover and refrigerate at least 1 hour before serving.

Käsekuchen

Käsekuchen is the traditional German version of cheesecake.

8 portions

The base	
6	tablespoons plus 1 teaspoon unsalted butter
1½	cups graham cracker crumbs
2	tablespoons sugar
1	teaspoon ground cinnamon

The filling	
½	lemon
2	eggs
⅓	cup sugar
¼	teaspoon salt
8	ounces cottage cheese
½	cup light cream
½	cup chopped mixed unsalted nuts

Preheat oven to 350°F. Coat an 8-inch round loose-bottomed cake pan with the 1 teaspoon butter. Melt the 6 tablespoons butter in a small saucepan over low heat. Add the crumbs, sugar and cinnamon; stir until the mixture is well combined and clings together. Reserving 2 tablespoons for the topping, press the mixture into the prepared pan. Grate the rind and squeeze the juice from the lemon half into a large bowl. Beat in the eggs, sugar and salt. Push the cottage cheese through a sieve and add along with the cream and half the nuts. Beat until the ingredients are well blended.

Spoon mixture into the prepared pan and smooth the top with a spatula. Sprinkle with the crumbs reserved from the base and remaining nuts. Bake on a rack in the middle level of the oven for 35 to 45 minutes, or until the filling has set and a cake tester inserted in the center of cake comes out clean. Turn off oven and let cake remain in it for 10 minutes. Remove cake from oven and transfer to wire rack to cool completely. Remove from pan. Refrigerate for at least 1 hour before serving.

Blueberry Cheese Tart

6 to 8 portions

The base

6	tablespoons plus 1 teaspoon unsalted butter	2	tablespoons sugar
1½	cups graham cracker crumbs	½	teaspoon ground cinnamon

The filling

8	ounces cottage cheese	⅓	cup sugar
8	ounces cream cheese, at room temperature	2	tablespoons creme de cassis
1	egg		

The topping

1	pint fresh blueberries	1	tablespoon water
2	tablespoons red-currant jelly		

Preheat oven to 350°F. Use the 1 teaspoon butter to coat an 8-inch tart pan. Melt the 6 tablespoons butter in a small saucepan over low heat. Add the crumbs, sugar and cinnamon; stir until mixture is well combined and it clings together. Press the crumbs into the bottom and up the sides of the tart pan. Bake in the middle level of the oven for 10 minutes. Remove from oven and allow to cool.

Increase oven heat to 375°F. Push the cottage cheese through a sieve into a medium-size bowl. Add the cream cheese, egg and sugar. Beat with a wooden spoon until well mixed. Add the crème de cassis and stir until blended. Spoon the filling into the crust, smoothing the top with a spatula. Bake 40 to 45 minutes, or until filling is firm. Remove tart from oven and allow to cool completely.

Wash the blueberries and set out on paper towels to dry. When the tart is cool, make a glaze by melting the red-currant jelly with the water in a small saucepan over low heat. Arrange the blueberries over the top of the tart. Spoon or brush the glaze over the top. Chill for at least 1 hour.

Berry Cheesecake

This can have a topping of any berry that is in season. The amount of sugar needed will vary with the type of berry; use a couple of tablespoons for sweet berries, ½ cup or more for cranberries.

12 portions

The base

6	tablespoons plus 1 teaspoon unsalted butter	1½	cups graham cracker crumbs
⅓	cup sugar		

The filling

1½	pounds cream cheese, at room temperature	4	eggs
⅔	cup sugar	1	lemon

The topping

2	teaspoons cornstarch	12	ounces berries
2	tablespoons to ½ cup sugar, depending on berries used	3	tablespoons water

Preheat oven to 350°F. Coat an 8-inch round loose-bottomed cake pan with the 1 teaspoon butter. Melt the 6 tablespoons butter in a small saucepan over low heat. Add the sugar and crumbs. Stir until the mixture is well combined and clings together when pressed. Press the mixture evenly over the bottom and halfway up the sides of the pan.

In a medium-size bowl beat the cream cheese until smooth. Beat in the sugar. Beat in the eggs, one at a time, beating well after each addition. Grate 2 teaspoons of lemon rind from the lemon. Add 1 teaspoon to the cheese mixture; reserve the second for the topping. Squeeze 1 teaspoon juice from the lemon; stir into the cheese mixture. Pour the cheese mixture into the lined cake pan. Bake on a rack in the middle level of the oven for 35 minutes. Turn off oven and leave

cheesecake in oven until cool. When cool, cover and refrigerate several hours or overnight.

To make the topping, combine the cornstarch, the required amount of sugar and berries in a medium-size saucepan. Add the water and the reserved lemon rind; stir to combine. Bring to a boil, then simmer over medium heat for 1 minute—1½ minutes for larger berries—stirring occasionally. Remove mixture from heat; set aside to cool. When cool, remove cake from refrigerator. If necessary, loosen cake from sides of pan with icing spatula or flexible-bladed knife. Remove cake from pan and carefully transfer to a serving plate. Spread the berry mixture evenly over the center, leaving a decorative rim of cheesecake.

Creamy Pineapple Cheesecake

12 portions

The filling

⅓	cup water
2	envelopes gelatin (2 scant tablespoons)
1	can crushed pineapple (1 pound 12 ounces)
12	ounces cream cheese, at room temperature
¼	cup sugar
1¼	cups heavy cream, chilled

The crust

4	tablespoons unsalted butter
1	cup graham cracker crumbs

The topping

8	canned pineapple rings, with their juice
4	large strawberries
1	tablespoon arrowroot

Put water in a small saucepan. Sprinkle on the gelatin; let stand 5 minutes. Place over low heat until gelatin becomes liquid, about 3 minutes. Cool slightly. Stir the crushed pineapple and its juice into the gelatin and set aside in a cool place until at the point of setting.

Combine the cream cheese and sugar in a large bowl; beat until smooth. Fold in the pineapple mixture. Whip the cream and fold in. Spoon the mixture into an 8-inch round springform pan. Smooth the top with a metal spatula.

Melt the butter in a small saucepan over low heat. Add the crumbs and stir until the mixture is well combined and clings together when pressed. Sprinkle crumb mixture over cheese filling, pressing down gently with a spatula. Cover and refrigerate for 3 hours.

Drain the pineapple rings, reserving ¾ cup juice. Wash, hull and halve the strawberries. Blend the arrowroot with 2 tablespoons of the reserved juice. Place arrowroot mixture and remaining juice in a small saucepan. Bring to a boil; simmer for 1 minute over medium heat. Cool.

If necessary, use an icing spatula or flexible-bladed knife to loosen cake from sides of pan. Release clip at side of pan and remove sides. Invert cheesecake onto serving plate. Arrange pineapple rings and strawberries in a decorative pattern on top of cake and spoon the glaze over top.

Red-Currant Refrigerator Cheesecake

This cheesecake works equally well with raspberries and strawberries.

6 portions

The base

8	tablespoons plus 1 teaspoon unsalted butter
2	cups graham cracker crumbs
1	teaspoon ground cinnamon

The topping

2	cups heavy cream
1	egg white

The filling

1¼	pounds red currants
¼	cup water
1	envelope gelatin (1 scant tablespoon)
1	pound cream cheese, at room temperature
¼	cup sugar
½	cup light cream

Lightly coat a 9-inch round loose-bottomed cake pan with the 1 teaspoon butter. Melt the remaining butter in a small saucepan set over low heat. Add the crumbs and cinnamon and stir until the mixture is well combined and clings together. Press crumbs evenly into the bottom of pan. Cover and refrigerate for 30 minutes or until set.

Wash the currants and set out on paper towels to dry. Place the water in a small saucepan. Sprinkle on the gelatin; let stand 5 minutes. Set over low heat until gelatin becomes liquid, about 3 minutes. Let cool slightly.

Beat the cream cheese and sugar together until smooth. Stir in the cream and 4 cups of the currants. Beat in the dissolved gelatin. Spoon into prepared pan. Cover and refrigerate 1 hour, or until the mixture has set.

In a large bowl beat the heavy cream until stiff peaks form. In another bowl beat the egg white until stiff but not dry (see Volume 9 Index). Fold the egg white into the cream. Spoon the cream mixture onto the cheesecake, making swirling patterns with the back of a spoon. Sprinkle remaining currants over the cream. Serve immediately or refrigerate until needed, up to 4 hours. Serve cold.

Orange Cheesecake with a Chocolate Crust

8 portions

The base

3	tablespoons unsalted butter
1½	ounces semisweet chocolate
1½	cups graham cracker crumbs

The topping

1	ounce semisweet chocolate

The filling

1	large orange
½	lemon
4	teaspoons gelatin
3	eggs
⅓	cup sugar
12	ounces cottage cheese
⅔	cup heavy cream

Melt the butter and chocolate together in a small saucepan set over low heat. Add the crumbs and stir until coated with chocolate. Press the mixture into the bottom of a buttered 8-inch round loose-bottomed cake pan. Chill at least 4 hours or overnight.

Grate the rind and squeeze the juices from the orange and lemon. Set the rind aside and place the juices in a small saucepan. Sprinkle the gelatin over the juices and let stand 5 minutes. Heat pan over very low heat until the gelatin becomes liquid, about 3 minutes; cool slightly. While the gelatin is melting, separate the eggs. Set the whites aside. Add the sugar to the yolks and whisk until thick, creamy and lemon-colored. Add the rind from the orange and lemon to the yolk mixture. Push the cottage cheese through a sieve and add.

Beat the egg mixture until smooth. Pour in the gelatin mixture in a thin stream, stirring constantly; set aside. Whip the cream until it just holds its shape. Fold into the cheese mixture. Whisk the egg whites until stiff but not dry (see Volume 9 Index). Stir one quarter of the whites into the cheese mixture and then fold in the rest. Spoon the mixture into the crumb base. Refrigerate several hours or overnight. When firm, loosen from sides with icing spatula or flexible-bladed knife. Remove pan and transfer cake to serving plate.

Melt the 1 ounce chocolate in a small bowl set over simmering water. Scrape the chocolate into a pastry bag fitted with a plain tip, or into a paper cone. Drizzle the chocolate over the top of the cheesecake in a decorative pattern. Allow to set.

Crostata di Ricotta

(Italian Cheese Pie)

8 portions

The pastry

12	tablespoons plus 1 teaspoon unsalted butter
2	cups all-purpose flour
¼	teaspoon salt
1	lemon
4	eggs
2	tablespoons sugar
5	tablespoons Marsala

The filling

4	eggs
2½	pounds ricotta cheese
2	lemons
1	orange
½	cup sugar
2	tablespoons all-purpose flour
¼	teaspoon salt
½	teaspoon vanilla extract
3	tablespoons raisins
2	tablespoons finely chopped candied peel
2	tablespoons slivered blanched almonds

Coat a 9-inch round springform pan with the 1 teaspoon butter; set aside. Cut the 12 tablespoons butter into small pieces. Sift the flour and salt into a large bowl; make a well in the center. Grate the rind of the lemon into the well. Separate the eggs, reserving the whites for another purpose. Add the butter, egg yolks, sugar and Marsala to the flour. Using your fingertips, blend all the ingredients together. Knead the dough lightly just until it is smooth and can be formed into a ball; do not overknead. Cover and refrigerate the dough until it is fairly firm, about 1 hour.

Break off about one quarter of the dough. Dust with flour, cover and return it to the refrigerator. Reshape the remaining dough into a ball. On a floured work surface, flatten the dough into a circle. Sprinkle flour over the top of the dough and roll out into a 12-inch circle. Lift the pastry onto the rolling pin and gently ease it into the springform pan so that it comes up about 1 inch on all sides. Cover lightly and refrigerate while you make the filling.

Preheat the oven to 350°F. Separate the eggs, reserving 3 of the whites for another purpose and setting 1 aside for lattice top. Place the ricotta in a medium-size bowl. Grate in the rind from the lemons and orange. Squeeze the juice from the lemons and add along with the sugar, flour, salt, vanilla extract and egg yolks. Beat until combined. Stir in the raisins and candied peel. Spoon the mixture into the prepared pastry case; smooth the top with a spatula. Sprinkle the top with the almonds.

Remove the reserved pastry from the refrigerator. Roll it out on a floured work surface to a rectangle at least 10 inches long. With a sharp knife cut the pastry into ½-inch-wide strips. Arrange over the top of filling to make a lattice pattern. Lightly crimp at sides to attach lattice to pastry base. Beat the egg white until foamy and brush the lattice with it. Bake the pie on a rack in the middle level of the oven for 1 hour, or until the crust is golden brown and the center is firm to the touch. Remove the pie from oven and place on a wire rack to cool. When cool, release clip at side of pan; remove sides. Transfer cheesecake to serving plate.

Yorkshire Cheesecakes

These traditional cakes, originally made with home-made curd cheese, are still popular today. Farmer or cottage cheese can be used.

24 2-inch cheesecakes

The base

2	teaspoons unsalted butter	1	recipe rich Short-Crust Pastry (see Volume 2 Index)

The filling

1	pound farmer or cottage cheese	½	teaspoon pumpkin pie spice
1	cup sugar	2	tablespoons currants
⅓	cup chopped mixed candied peel	4	tablespoons unsalted butter
		2	eggs

Preheat the oven to 350°F. Coat 24 2-inch tartlet pans with the 2 teaspoons butter; set aside. On a lightly floured work surface, roll out the short-crust pastry to a circle about ⅛ inch thick. Using a 3-inch round pastry cutter, cut out 24 circles, rerolling scraps as necessary. Place a circle of pastry in each pan, easing it into bottom and up sides. Place pans on a baking sheet and refrigerate while you make the filling.

Press the cheese through a sieve into a medium-size bowl. Add the sugar, candied peel, spice and currants; stir until combined. In a small saucepan, melt the 4 tablespoons butter over low heat. Beat the eggs lightly. Add to cheese mixture along with melted butter; beat until well blended. Divide the cheese mixture evenly among the pastry cases. Smooth the tops with a small spatula. Bake on a rack in the middle level of the oven for 15 to 20 minutes, or until the cheesecakes are golden brown on top.

Remove pans from oven. While still warm, use a thin-bladed knife to remove. Place cakes on a wire rack to cool before serving. Yorkshire cheesecakes are traditionally eaten at room temperature.

Refrigerator Lemon Cheesecake

8 portions

The base

½	recipe Whole Egg Spongecake (see Volume 8 Index), baked in an 8-inch springform pan*

The topping

confectioner's sugar

The filling

¼	cup water
1	envelope gelatin (1 scant tablespoon)
3	eggs
½	cup plus 2 tablespoons sugar
¼	teaspoon salt
¼	cup milk
1	lemon
12	ounces cottage cheese
⅔	cup heavy cream

Split the spongecake crosswise into two layers. Placing the cut-side up, lay one layer in an 8-inch springform pan.

*Spongecakes freeze well, so if you prefer, make one recipe of Whole-Egg Spongecake instead of a half recipe, and freeze the remaining layer.

Place the water in a small saucepan. Sprinkle on the gelatin; let stand 5 minutes. Set over very low heat until gelatin becomes liquid, about 3 minutes. Cool slightly. Separate 2 of the eggs, setting whites aside in a large bowl, and placing yolks in a medium-size saucepan. To egg yolks, add remaining whole egg, ½ cup of the sugar, the salt and milk;

beat together until combined. Cook over low heat, stirring constantly, for 3 to 4 minutes, or just until the custard thickens. Do not allow the custard to come to a boil or it will curdle. Remove the pan from the heat and stir in the dissolved gelatin. Set the pan aside until the custard has cooled to room temperature.

Grate the rind and squeeze the juice from the lemon. Sieve the cottage cheese. Add the rind and cottage cheese to the custard mixture along with the remaining 2 tablespoons sugar. Whip the cream until soft peaks form; fold into the mixture. Beat the egg whites until stiff but not dry (see Volume 9 Index). Stir one quarter of them into the mixture and then fold in the rest. Gently spoon the mixture onto the prepared spongecake and smooth the top with a spatula. Cover with remaining half layer, turned cut-side down and refrigerate for at least 2 hours, or until set.

When cheesecake is set, release clip and remove sides of pan. Dust cheesecake with confectioner's sugar and transfer to serving plate. Serve cut into wedges.

Part Five

A "JUST DESSERTS" PARTY FOR TWELVE

Not only is there always room for dessert, but when the pastry cart comes around at the end of the meal, which of us has not wanted—but been too embarrassed to ask for—some of everything, please. Although there are people who claim not to like dessert, they are far outnumbered by those for whom the last course is the whole point of the meal, indeed of the day. Merely the thought of Mom's apple pie, *tarte aux pommes,* or *Apfelstrudel* is enough to make most bellies growl with desire. And is there anyone who doesn't have memories of standing wistful and fidgety at a bakery window, allowance long since spent, as each bang of the door sent teasing gusts of sugar-and-spice-scented air into the street. Your friends will love you for having a dessert party, which for all its surface chic—and it can be very chic indeed—satisfies some primitive, forever-hungry place within all of us.

To best prepare for this party, therefore, think of it as a masquerade that your friends will attend looking their most beautiful and swank, while deep inside them lurk little boys and girls with chocolate-milk moustaches. Despite stout-hearted attempts not to, they will inexorably be drawn back to the dessert table to have "just a smidgin" more, so always provide an abundance of food, more than you think your guests could ever eat, for they will astonish you. Keeping in mind what readying such bounty entails, we have chosen desserts that can—at least in part and sometimes completely—be prepared ahead of time. The brioche, the pie dough, and the puff pastry can all be made in advance and refrigerated until you are ready to continue with the recipe; both the Florentines and the brandy snaps can be made a day or two ahead and stored airtight (fill the brandy snaps just before serving); and the *coeur à la crème* (a delicate, crustless cheesecake), the devil's food cake, the gâteau, and the cold raspberry soufflé actually *must* be made in advance. We have even provided a recipe for make-ahead whipped cream.

For this buffet party to be truly stunning, play some Fred Astaire recordings and . . . put on the ritz. Set your table with a luxurious lace cloth, your best china and silver—don't forget the coffee cups—and a dozen gleaming brandy snifters for your guests to settle back with when the eating is done. Tie the napkins with lace edging—available by the yard in trimming stores—and light the table with clusters of candles set in crystal or glass holders. If you are feeling playful, consider doing these table appointments in icing colors—pale pink, white, sky blue, lemon—and choose an assortment of flowers in these or similarly delicate hues—lacy white lilacs, yellow freesias, peach-colored roses, or masses of baby's breath and forget-me-nots. Nestle the desserts together or scatter them, but take care to display them so they best complement one another and the setting. Then, when everything is arranged so it dazzles the eye, greet your guests in the certain knowledge that while they are exchanging pleasantries with you, even the most abstemious and elegant among them will be wishing they could pole vault to the table.

DESSERT PARTY FOR TWELVE

Brioche Bread Pudding with Whiskey or Apricot Sauce

Devil's Food Cake

(See Volume 1 Index)

Cold Raspberry Soufflé

Puff Pastry Tart with Glazed Grapes

Gâteau au Citron

(See Volume 1 Index)

Coeur à la Crème with Kiwi Fruit

Chocolate Mousse

Florentines and Brandy Snaps Filled with Whipped Cream

(See Volume 3 Index)

Latticed Apple Pie

(See Volume 2 Index)

Oranges and Strawberries in Orange Liqueur

Brandies

Brandy, the most esteemed of all after-dinner drinks, is made almost wherever wine grapes are grown. Although the two greatest brandies of France—Cognac and Armagnac—are indisputably the two greatest brandies in the world, the less celebrated but still fine brandies of France have their counterparts in America, Spain, Italy, Greece, Mexico, Russia, and even Peru, which has been producing pisco (perhaps best known in the notoriously potent Pisco Sour) for more than 300 years. It is the Dutch, however, whom legend credits with the invention of this distilled wine, and it is the Dutch word "brandewijn" (burnt wine) that gave brandy its name.

The French and American brandies served as the grace note of this dessert party are pleasingly diverse in taste, ranging from the mellowness and depth of a great Cognac to the fruitier nuances of a California brandy. Courvoisier, Hennessy, Martell, and Remy Martin are all held in great repute by Cognac connoisseurs and Marquis de Caussade and the 10-year-old Marquis de Montesquiou are fine examples—albeit very different—of the earthy richness of an Armagnac. For good French brandies in the inexpensive price range, try Rothschild V.S.O.P. or Raynal. American brandies, too, have a quality very much their own and are well worth investigating. Christian Brothers and E. & J. Brandy are two of the best known.

Market List

Fruits and Vegetables

2	pounds cooking apples	8	large seedless oranges	3	large lemons
½	pound seedless grapes, preferably red	2	pints raspberries or three 10-ounce packages frozen	2	pints strawberries small bunch mint (optional)
4	or 5 kiwi fruit				

Dairy

5	pounds unsalted butter	1	pint half-and-half (or 1 cup milk and 1 cup light cream)	8	ounces cream cheese
½	pint light cream			8	ounces cottage cheese
2	quarts heavy cream	1	cup sour cream	32	large eggs
				5¼	cups milk

Specialty Items

¾	cup slivered blanched almonds	12	ounces semisweet chocolate	6	ounces chocolate chips crystallized violets or pistachio nuts
¼	cup glacéed cherries	4	ounces unsweetened chocolate		

Staples

Baking powder
Baking soda
Cornstarch
Cream of tartar
Flour
Gelatin
Cognac or rum

Grand Marnier, Cointreau, or curacao
Bourbon or Scotch
Honey
Light molasses or dark molasses and corn syrup
Apricot preserves
Golden raisins

Dark raisins
Salt
Vanilla extract
Vegetable shortening or lard
Confectioners' sugar
Granulated sugar
Dark brown sugar

106

Brioche Bread Pudding

10 portions

1	cup dark raisins	4	cups milk
1	loaf Brioche (1½ pounds)	2	cups heavy cream
	(see Volume 7 Index)	8	eggs
8	tablespoons unsalted butter	1	cup sugar
½	teaspoon cinnamon	2	teaspoons vanilla extract
	(optional)		

Preheat the broiler. Steam the raisins over boiling water for about 10 minutes to plump them. Pat them dry.

Trim the crusts from the brioche loaf and cut loaf into thin slices. There should be about 20 slices. Butter them well and stack them in piles of 4 or 5. Cut each pile in half diagonally to make triangles. Spread the triangles in a single layer, buttered side up, on cookie sheets and put under the broiler about 5 inches from the heat source for 2 minutes, until they are golden and barely crisp.

Lightly butter a large shallow ovenproof dish. Arrange the brioche, toasted side up, in overlapping slices with the points of the triangles up. Sprinkle the raisins over the slices and dust with cinnamon.

Combine the milk and cream and heat to just below a boil. Separate 2 of the eggs, reserving whites for another purpose. In a large bowl beat the yolks and whole eggs together lightly but thoroughly. Stir in the sugar. Gradually add the hot milk mixture in a thin stream, stirring constantly until the milk is incorporated and the sugar is dissolved. Add the vanilla extract. Pour the mixture over the bread slices, holding them in place with a spatula. Set dish aside for about 30 minutes.

Preheat the oven to 350°F. Set the baking dish in a larger pan. Pour enough hot water into the larger pan to come halfway up the sides of the baking dish. Bake for about 40 minutes, or until a knife inserted in the center comes out clean.

Serve warm or at room temperature with Whiskey Sauce or Apricot Sauce (recipes follow). Brioche can be baked in advance in a 6-cup loaf pan or Pullman loaf pan. Do not use egg glaze for this recipe.

Whiskey Sauce

makes about 2½ cups

2	cups half-and-half, or 1 cup		pinch of salt
	milk combined with 1	⅓	cup dark brown sugar
	cup light cream	¼	cup bourbon or Scotch
4	eggs		whiskey

In a small pan scald the half-and-half by bringing it almost to a boil. Separate the eggs, reserving the whites for another use. In the top of a double boiler, beat the egg yolks with the salt and sugar until thick, smooth, and lemon-colored. Stirring constantly, gradually add the scalded half-and-half.

Place the pan over, but not in, boiling water and cook, stirring constantly, until the sauce is thick enough to coat a spoon (180°F on a candy thermometer).

Remove the sauce from the heat and stir in the whiskey. Strain into a serving bowl and refrigerate. Serve cold.

Apricot Sauce

makes about 1 cup

1	cup apricot preserves	¼	cup brandy or rum
1	tablespoon water		

In a small pan, bring the apricot preserves and the water just to a boil, stirring often. Immediately remove from the heat and force through a sieve into a serving bowl. Stir in the brandy or rum. Serve warm or at room temperature.

Cold Raspberry Soufflé

8 portions

2	pints fresh raspberries, or 3 packages (10 ounces) frozen raspberries, thawed
7	eggs
½	cup sugar
1	lemon

2	tablespoons cold water
2	envelopes gelatin (2 scant tablespoons)
1	cup heavy cream
	crystallized violets or pistachio nuts for garnish (optional)

Prepare a collar for a 6-cup soufflé dish (see Volume 9 Index).

Wash the raspberries and drain them. Purée and strain to remove seeds. If using frozen berries, reserve ⅓ cup of juice.

Separate 4 of the eggs, reserving the whites for another use. Beat the whole eggs and egg yolks with the sugar until thick and light in color. Juice the lemon to measure 1 tablespoon. If using, combine the reserved raspberry juice with the lemon juice and water. If not using, add another ⅓ cup water. Sprinkle the gelatin over it and let stand 5 minutes. Place bowl in a pan of hot water set over low heat and stir to dissolve completely. Beat the cream until soft peaks form. Fold into the raspberry purée.

Pour into the prepared soufflé dish and chill for at least 5 hours but no longer than 12.

Remove collar. Garnish top of the soufflé with crystallized violets or chopped green pistachio nuts and serve at once.

Make-Ahead Whipped Cream

makes about 4 cups

2	cups heavy cream
¼	cup granulated sugar

2	teaspoons vanilla extract

Be sure cream, beater and bowl are very cold. Whip the cream, adding the sugar gradually, until soft peaks form. Stir in the vanilla.

Turn the cream into a strainer that has been lined with three layers of dampened cheesecloth or a large coffee filter. Set the lined strainer over a deep bowl, making sure the bottom of the strainer clears the bottom of the bowl. Cover the strainer with plastic wrap and refrigerate the bowl and strainer. The whipped cream can be prepared up to 12 hours ahead.

108

Puff Pastry Tart with Glazed Grapes

8 to 10 portions

1 rectangular Puff Pastry
tranche, 7 × 12 inches
(see Volume 5 Index),
baked, at room temperature

2 cups Crème Pâtissière (see
Volume 5 Index)
½ pound seedless grapes, preferably red
2 tablespoons apricot preserves

Prepare the puff pastry tart as directed. Before baking, prick the surface thoroughly with the tines of a fork. Allow the tart to cool completely before filling it.

Shortly before serving, fill the baked and cooled tart with the crème pâtissière, smoothing it with a spatula.

Wash, dry and halve the grapes lengthwise. Place them flat side down in a decorative pattern on top of the crème patissière.

In a small pan, melt the preserves with 1 tablespoon water and bring to a boil. Immediately remove from the heat and force through a sieve into a small bowl. Carefully brush the mixture on the grapes to glaze them.

Cœur à la Crème with Kiwi Fruit

6 to 8 portions

8 ounces cottage cheese
8 ounces cream cheese
1 cup heavy cream

confectioners' sugar
(optional)
4 or 5 kiwi fruit

With the back of a spoon, push the cottage cheese through a fine strainer into a mixing bowl. Add the cream cheese and, with rotary or hand-held electric beater, beat the cheeses together until smooth. Whip the cream until stiff and fold it into the cheese mixture. If desired, add sugar to taste.

Line a 3-cup heart-shaped perforated mold with a large piece of cheesecloth, doubled, that has been rinsed in cold water and wrung out.

Turn the cheese mixture into the mold, and fold the ends of the cheesecloth up over the top. Cover the mold with plastic or foil. Suspend the mold over a bowl so that the whey drips into the bowl. Refrigerate overnight.

When ready to serve, uncover and invert the mold onto a serving dish. Peel and thinly slice the kiwi fruit. Surround the heart with sliced kiwis and place a single flower diagonally across the top.

Oranges and Strawberries in Orange Liqueur

8 to 10 portions

8 large seedless navel oranges
2 pints ripe strawberries
2 to 4 tablespoons sugar

¼ cup Grand Marnier,
Cointreau or curaçao
fresh mint leaves

Peel the oranges, removing all the white pith, and cut them horizontally into ½-inch slices. Cut the slices in half cross-wise.

Wash and hull the strawberries. Reserve a few small ones for the top of the dish. Cut remaining strawberries in half or in thirds, depending on their size. Add sugar to the strawberries—according to taste—and let them sit for a few minutes.

Combine the orange slices and strawberries in a glass serving bowl. Pour the orange liqueur over them, toss gently and place the reserved whole berries on top.

Cover and chill for ½ hour. Serve immediately, garnished with a few mint leaves.

Chocolate Mousse

8 portions

6 eggs
½ cup heavy cream
8 ounces semisweet chocolate
3 tablespoons hot water
3 tablespoons Cognac, rum or Grand Marnier

pinch of salt
pinch of cream of tartar
3 tablespoons sugar
4 cups whipped cream (see Index)

Separate the eggs. Place the cream in the top part of a double boiler set over simmering water. Break the chocolate into pieces and add. Stir occasionally until chocolate is melted. Add the hot water and continue to cook, stirring, until the mixture is smooth. Add the egg yolks, one at a time, beating well after each addition. Remove the mixture from the heat and stir in the Cognac.

Beat the whites with a pinch of salt and cream of tartar until soft peaks form. Continue to beat, while gradually adding the sugar, until the whites form stiff peaks (see Volume 9 Index).

Stir about one quarter of the beaten whites into the chocolate mixture to lighten it. Then fold in the balance of the whites.

Turn the mousse into a serving bowl, cover, and chill it for 12 hours. Serve accompanied by a bowl of whipped cream.

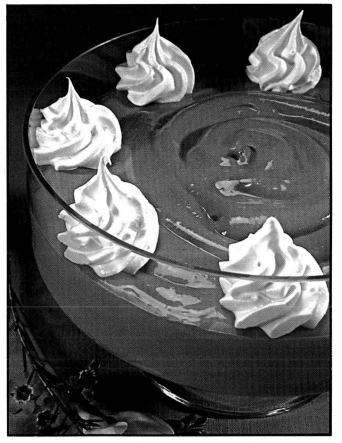

INDEX